HACKS FOR

PUBG

PLAYERS

HACKS FOR
PUBG
PLAYERS

AN UNOFFICIAL GAMER'S GUIDE

JASON R. RICH

Racehorse Publishing

CONTENTS

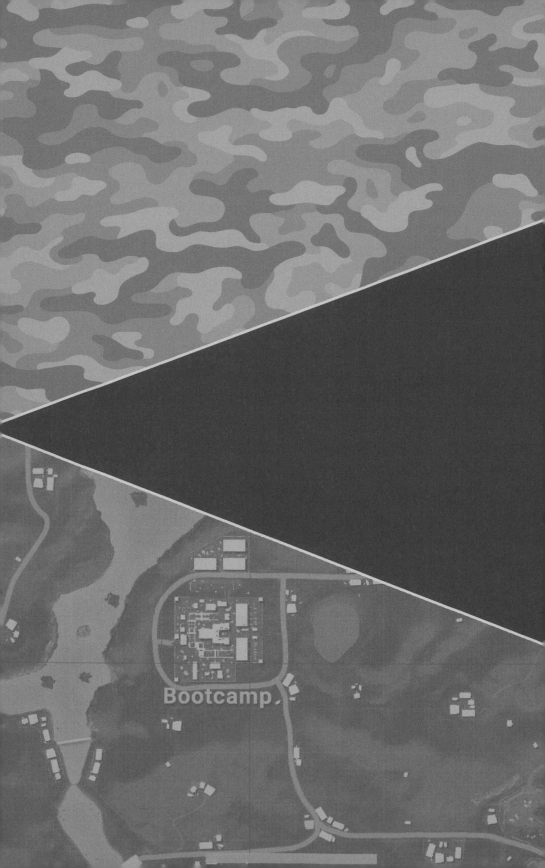

SECTION 1

INTRODUCTION TO PUBG

GET READY TO EXPERIENCE A HIGH-ACTION, REAL-TIME, COMBAT-ORIENTED battle royale game that'll pit you against up to 99 other players, all of whom have just one primary objective—to become the last person alive at the end of each match. This objective is achieved by killing off *all* of your adversaries.

You're about to enter an intense adventure where you control a single soldier who gets airlifted to a remote island. Your soldier must fight for survival against other highly skilled and potentially well-armed soldiers, each of whom is controlled in real-time by another gamer.

As you're about to discover, *PUBG* is a very difficult game to master, because in addition to all the challenges built into the game, you also must contend with the real-time actions of other gamers, who will frequently alter their fighting or defensive strategies in an attempt to outsmart and kill you.

PlayerUnknown's Battlegrounds, also known simply as ***PUBG***, has become one of the most popular combat games in the world. It can be played on a PC, Playstation 4, Xbox One, iPhone, iPad, or on many Android-based mobile devices.

PUBG'S MAIN GAME PLAY MODES

Whether you want to experience *PUBG* alone or with one or several online friends, a handful of different game play modes are available from the game's Play menu. Along with the following types of **Public Match** options, there's also the **Custom Match** option.

The **Training Mode** will help you learn and practice basic combat techniques before entering into matches. Each time you enter into Training Mode, you have 30 minutes to collect and experiment with different types of weapons, weapon attachments, items, and armor in a handful of different shooting range and obstacle course scenarios.

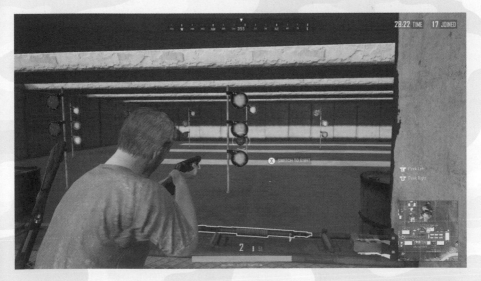

Training Mode is ideal for beginners. One of the keys to becoming good at playing *PUBG* and surviving during matches is being able to successfully work with the different types of weapons, ammo, tools, armor, and vehicles that you'll discover upon arriving on the island. Training Mode allows you to practice using weapons in a non-lethal environment.

While in Training Mode, walk up to one of these shooting ranges, pick up a weapon and compatible ammo, and then practice your aim and shooting skills. Practice shooting at moving targets from a distance, so when you participate in an actual match, you'll already have the core skills needed to achieve head shots, even if your target is in motion.

There are several game play modes that allow you to experience actual matches. Select the **Play** option, and then choose between the **Solo** (TPP or FPP), **Duo**, **Squad,** or **1-Man-Squad** game play modes.

- **Solo** mode pits your soldier against up to 99 enemies. TPP stands for Third Person Perspective and FPP stands for First Person Perspective.
- **Duo** mode allows you to team up with one other gamer. Together, you must kill off up to 98 adversaries in order to win each match.
- Groups of up to four gamers each work together as a team when you select **Squad** mode. The goal is still to become the last soldier standing, but you can work with other gamers who can heal each other, protect each other, share weapons and items, and work together to launch coordinated attacks. After selecting Squad mode, you can choose the Auto Matching feature to have the game randomly match you up with random players (strangers) or select and invite specific players (online friends) to join your squad.
- The **1-Man-Squad** mode allows you to experience a *PUBG* match alone, but you'll encounter teams of two, three, or four gamers (squads) working together. This makes being a solo player more challenging, since multiple enemies will gang up on you during firefights.

Regardless of which gaming system you use and which gaming play mode you select, a continuous, high-speed Internet connection is always required to play *PUBG*. Having the fastest possible Internet connection will give you an edge, as even a fraction of a second delay or Internet connection glitch could mean the difference between survival and sudden death during a match.

Custom Matches allow you to create a specialized type of match to experience when playing *PUBG*, and then invite your online friends (and/or random *PUBG* players) to participate. This is functionality that's relatively new to the game, and the features it offers have been evolving and expanding on a pretty regular basis. Once you choose the Custom Match option from the menu displayed on the Lobby screen, select between Normal Mode, Zombie Mode, War Mode, or ESports Mode.

From the Custom Matches menu, you're able to join a match that's already been created by someone else or choose the Create option to create your own customized match experience. For the latest details on Custom Matches, visit: https://support.pubg.com /hc/en-us/articles/260007290113-What-are-custom-matches.

HOW TO PURCHASE AND DOWNLOAD *PUBG*

Regardless of which gaming platform you use to experience *PUBG*, the actual game play is very similar, although as you'll soon discover, how the game screen looks varies slightly in each version. The price of the game varies, but for the core game, plan on spending about $30.00 (US) for the PC, PS4, or Xbox One version. The mobile version of *PUBG* is free, but in-app purchases are required to acquire a Season Pass and other game content.

A retail version of *PUBG* is sold in stores that sell computer and video games; however, once you purchase the game at your favorite store, you'll still need to download and install the entire game via the Internet, as updated versions of *PUBG* are released on a regular basis.

The retail versions include a bundle of additional content, such as a Season Pass, Crates, Items, and in-game currency that can be used to acquire additional items. The alternative is to purchase the game online and then download it directly to your computer or console-based system.

To purchase the PC version of the game, launch your favorite web browser and visit **www. pubg.com**. Click on the **Buy Now** button that's displayed in the top-right corner of the screen. You'll be able to purchase the core game, or a bundle pack that includes a Season Pass or a Season Pass along with downloadable content for the game.

The Xbox One version of *PUBG* is available online from the **Microsoft Store** (www.xbox.com/en-US/games/playerunknowns -battlegrounds#purchaseoptions), while the PlayStation 4 version is available from the **PlayStation Store** (https://store.playstation .com/en-us/product/UP5082-CUSA14081_00-PTSBUN0000000000).

The iOS (iPhone/iPad) version of *PUBG* **Mobile** is available from the **App Store**, and the Android-based version of the game can be purchased and acquired from the **Google Play Store**. For more information about *PUBG* Mobile, visit **www.pubgmobile .com**.

PUBG BASICS YOU MUST UNDERSTAND

It's essential that you understand all of the game's elements and nuances, and how everything interrelates. *PUBG* is much more than a shooting game!

After choosing a game play mode, each match begins in the pre-deployment area, as all soldiers wait to board the aircraft that transports everyone to the island. If you're playing a Duo or Squad match, for example, this is where you can meet up with your partner or squad mates for the first time in the game before a match.

As the aircraft flies over the island, each player, duo, or squad must choose the ideal time to leap from the plane and freefall toward land. Notice the seat layout of the airplane in the bottom-left corner of the screen. At the start of the flight, all seats are full and displayed in yellow. When soldiers begin jumping off the airplane, their seats will be vacated. This too is displayed on the seating chart. Keep an eye on this display to inform you when the majority of your enemies are leaving the aircraft.

By switching to the Island Map, you'll see a detailed overview of the island and discover its various points of interest. Depending on the strategy you choose to adopt, you might want to land in the heart of a popular area, where you're virtually guaranteed to encounter enemy soldiers almost immediately. An alternate strategy is to land in a more remote area, build up your soldier's arsenal, and then seek out combat situations.

You're able to zoom in and out on the map and scroll around to see specific locations in greater detail. Weapons, ammo, armor, and weapon attachments are more apt to be found within buildings and structures. When choosing a landing spot, choose one that's close to buildings or structures where you'll likely be able to quickly arm your soldier and take cover.

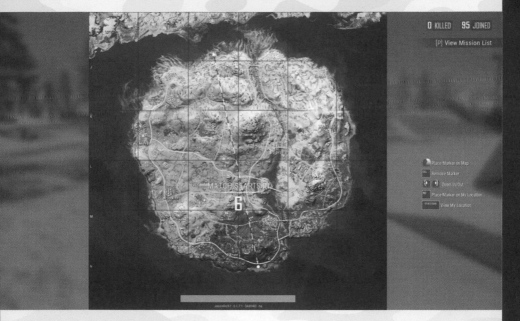

While in the pre-deployment area, or for a short time after the aircraft departs, a line appears on the Island Map that depicts the random route the aircraft will follow over the island. Use this route information to help you choose an ideal landing spot.

Upon leaping from the aircraft, use your controller or keyboard/mouse controls to point your soldier straight downward to boost their falling speed and reach land faster. Soldiers can fall at a maximum speed of 232 kilometers per second.

During freefall, keep your soldier's body parallel to the land below to reduce their rate of descent. Using the controls, you're able to help them glide across vast distances before their parachute automatically deploys. The gauge displayed near the bottom-left corner of the screen shows how quickly your soldier is falling.

As your soldier gets close to land, their parachute automatically opens and slows down their fall speed. During this time, you have more precise navigational control. However, you can choose to deploy the parachute at any time once your soldier leaps from the aircraft.

The moment you land on the island, you'll discover your soldier is unarmed and vulnerable to attack. Your first objective is to get to a safe location, and then begin searching the immediate area for armor, weapons, weapon enhancements, tools, and compatible ammo. Without these items, all you can do is move around and throw punches, which are no match against any type of weapon.

Especially if you're a newb (beginner), avoid landing in a highly congested and popular area and engaging in combat right away. You're better off choosing a more remote location and building up your arsenal before your soldier is forced to fight.

To cover a lot of territory while freefalling, open your parachute early so you can glide more slowly toward land and have more precise navigational control. The drawback is that you'll reach land a lot slower and the soldiers that beat you to your chosen landing location could collect all of the best weapons, ammo, armor, and other items before you arrive.

Once you choose a landing location, it's a good strategy to get there as quickly as possible—before your enemies—so you can grab weapons and ammo, and then position yourself to defend yourself or launch attacks as needed, based on how close your enemies land.

Initially, you'll need to walk, run, or crawl around to reach a safe area of the island. Your soldier can also jump or climb, as needed, or ride in certain types of vehicles to get around faster. Anytime you're in an open area, keep moving in an unpredictable, zig-zag pattern, and simultaneously jump repeatedly to make yourself a moving target that's more difficult for enemies to hit.

Whenever necessary, use the terrain around you for protection. Crouching behind a rock or solid structure, for example, offers better protection than hiding behind an object that doesn't protect your soldier's entire body or that can easily be destroyed by an enemy's weapon.

In addition to having access to many different types of guns, throwable weapons (and throwable explosive weapons) can be found and used on the island. Some of the throwable weapons include: Apples, Smoke Grenades, Snowballs, Stun Grenades, Molotov Cocktails, and Frag Grenades.

Keep in mind, throwable weapons can bounce upon landing, plus they'll often bounce off of a solid object (such as a wall). Each of these throwable items work differently in combat. Some will distract an enemy but cause little or no harm, while others, like a Frag Grenade, can be deadly if used correctly from an appropriate distance.

If you opt to use a Flash Grenade, right before it detonates, have your soldier look away, so he/she is not at all impacted by the loud and bright blast. This is particularly important if you're close to the spot it detonates.

On the island, there are many types of weapons, weapon enhancements, and tools you can use to defeat your enemies and stay alive longer. Ultimately, you'll need to learn where to find the best weapons and discover how to use them. Plus, you'll need to collect and have on hand the correct type of ammo for the weapon you're attempting to use. After all, a weapon without compatible ammunition is utterly useless.

In addition to weapons, there are many types of weapon enhancements that can be found and collected separately that'll make a weapon more powerful. For example, there are different types of scopes that can be added to certain weapons. These allow you to more accurately aim at targets far off in the distance.

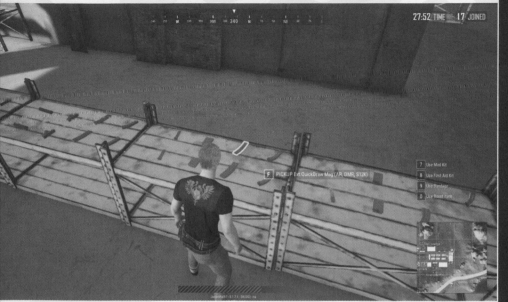

Each type of gun takes a different amount of time to reload, and each can hold a different number of bullets. Adding a Stock or Magazine to certain types of weapons allow them to hold more bullets, while Grips or Muzzles, for example, will increase shooting accuracy or make a weapon easier to handle. A Muzzle reduces the noise generated by a gun, while a Scope improves its aiming accuracy.

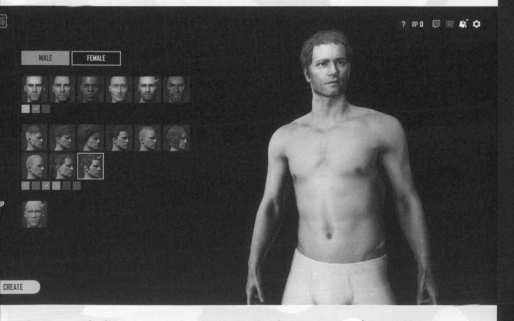

Prior to a match, there are many ways to customize the appearance of your soldier. Some outfits and accessories are included with the game, but most need to be purchased or unlocked by completing specific objectives. These customizations are for **cosmetic purposes only.** They have no impact on your soldier's strength or speed, nor do they offer any defensive protection or offensive advantage in combat situations.

Once your soldier lands on the island, this is when you'll need to find, pick up, and opt to use different types of armor and tools that'll make your soldier able to better withstand the negative impact of attacks. A soldier's armor can include a Helmet and Vest. There are three levels of each type of armor. The higher the level, the more protection it offers. Shown here, the soldier grabs and then puts on a Level 1 Helmet.

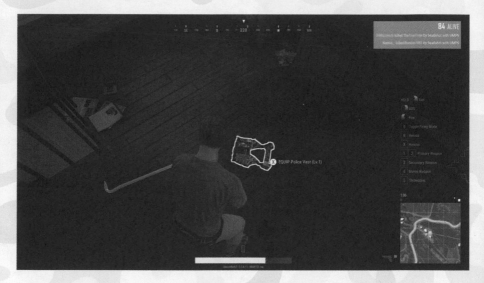

A **Level 1** Vest (shown) or Helmet offers 30 percent damage reduction resulting from an attack or bullet hit. A **Level 2** Vest or Helmet offers 40 percent damage reduction resulting from an attack or bullet hit. A **Level 3** Vest or Helmet offers a 55 percent damage reduction resulting from an attack or bullet hit.

Early on during a match, you also need to find and grab a Backpack for your soldier. These too have three levels, which determines how much stuff it can hold.

The terrain on the island varies a lot, so you need to be able to safely navigate around and use the terrain to your advantage whenever possible. *PUBG* matches can take place in one of several locations, including Erangel, Miramar, Sanhok, and Vikendi.

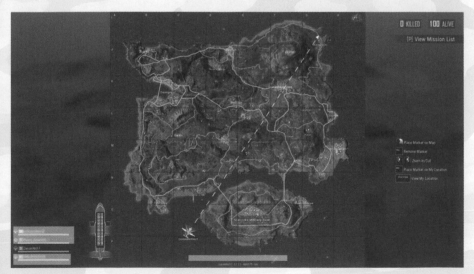

Each location offers different types of terrain and unique points of interest to explore. New locations are periodically added to *PUBG*, and changes are sometimes made to existing locations. It's important to study each of the maps, so you become familiar with the various places you may be visiting and understand what unique challenges and opportunities each different type of terrain offers during combat situations. Shown here is the Erangel map.

Shown here is the Miramar island map.

The Sanhok island map is shown here.

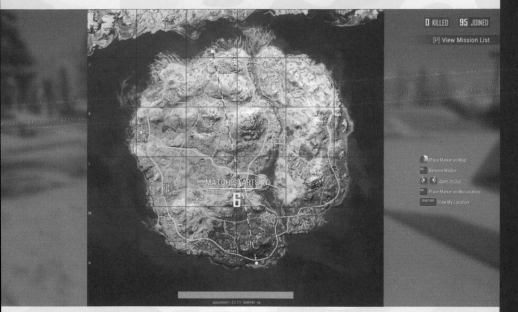

Check out the Vikendi island map.

STAY ON THE SAFE SIDE OF THE BLUE WALL AND WITHIN THE CIRCLE

Once a match begins, the safe area of the island will slowly shrink. Don't get caught far away from the inner circle, or you could find yourself having to travel great distances in order to survive and reach the safe area of the island. Without hopping into a vehicle, this could quickly become a losing proposition.

Choosing a good landing spot after leaping from the plane is one of the first decisions you'll make during a match, and it's also one of the most important. Your landing spot determines what strategies you'll need to implement right away in order to survive. This decision often impacts how quickly you'll be confronted by enemy attacks.

In addition to having to contend with many different types of terrain, and up to 99 other enemy soldiers, *PUBG* throws in another ongoing obstacle–the **blue wall**. Shortly after each match begins, a blue wall takes on a circular shape and begins forming, moving, and expanding at a steady pace. It's imperative that you stay within the safe circle, on the *inside* of the blue wall.

For every second you're on the wrong side of the blue wall, your soldier's health gets depleted. When your soldier's Health meter reaches zero, he or she dies. You're immediately removed from the match upon death. Use the map screen or the mini-map displayed in the bottom-right corner of the screen to help you determine where the blue wall is and what direction you need to travel in order to reach the safe zone using the most direct route possible.

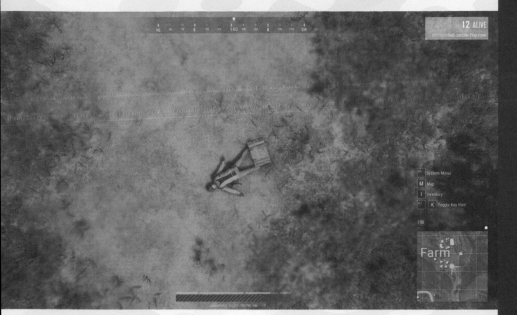

Aside from the blue wall, there are many other ways to die during a match. You can be shot at, killed by an explosive weapon, receive fatal damage within the Red Zone, or get badly injured resulting from a fall, for example.

During each match, be sure to pick up Health-related items that allow you to restore some or all of your health after receiving an injury. Using **Bandages**, **First Aid Kits**, and **Medkits** are examples of items that'll help you heal your soldier during a match and replenish some or all of their Health meter. As you'll discover, each item is used slightly differently and takes a different amount of time to work.

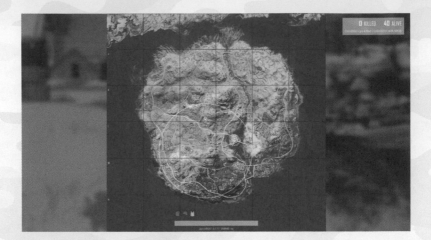

As the blue wall expands, all surviving soldiers are forced into a smaller and smaller "safe area," on the island, which pushes everyone into closer proximity. If you manage to survive until the later stages of a match, you'll need to defend yourself and kill off your enemies before they find and kill you. Remember, there can only be one survivor at the end of each Solo match. (If you're playing a Duos or Squad match, you and your partner or team mates could theoretically become the last soldiers alive on the island when you win a match.)

BEWARE OF THE RED ZONE

During every match, also stay clear of the **Red Zone**! This is an area of the map that's selected randomly after a match begins. If your soldier gets caught in the Red Zone, he'll receive major Health damage that'll cause death unless you exit the area very quickly or take shelter.

If you get stuck in a Red Zone area, get into a building fast for safety. Hiding within a vehicle won't offer protection. However, riding within a vehicle could help you exit the Red Zone area quickly before the storm of deadly explosions begin.

WAYS TO BUILD UP YOUR SOLDIER'S ARSENAL

One of the keys to success when playing *PUBG* is to quickly build up your soldier's arsenal, collect ammo, and then continuously work to improve that arsenal by collecting more powerful weapons, weapon enhancements (Scopes, Magazines, Muzzles, Grips, and Stocks), and compatible ammo. There are several ways to collect weapons (and ammo) during a match.

Each time you hit an enemy with a bullet or injure but don't kill them, this is referred to as a "knock." Sometimes leaving your "knocks" alone will cause other enemies to approach and finish off the kill. When they approach, you can shoot and kill them as well, and then collect the loot from two or more enemies, instead of just one.

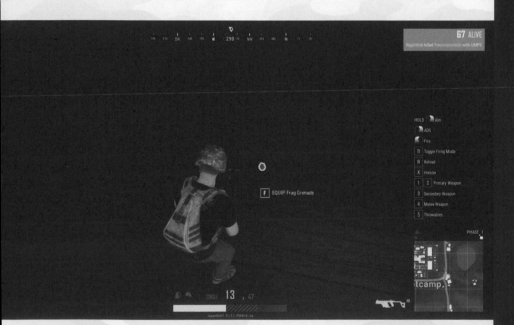

As you're exploring the inside of a structure or building, you'll often find weapons and ammo lying on the ground, out in the open, which your soldier can pick up. Here a Frag Grenade is about to be picked up by the soldier and placed within his inventory.

Anytime you kill an enemy, you have the option (if it's safe) to approach their corpse and pick up the weapons, ammo, and items the now-dead soldier was carrying.

Crate Drops are another way to quickly gather a selection of high-end gear. Randomly during a match, a crate will fall from the sky. Listen for an airplane to fly overhead during a match. Look up and you'll sometimes see a crate falling from the sky that's attached to a parachute. The crate falls slowly once the parachute deploys, and all soldiers in the area will see it.

Crate Drops often contain level-3 armor and Backpacks, along with powerful weapons and useful weapon enhancements, like Scopes. Notice the Crate Drop and its parachute (about to land on the ground) directly in front of the vehicle. As soon as it lands, the crate emits an attention-getting burst of bright red smoke.

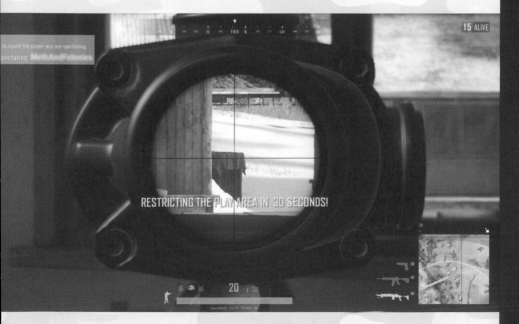

It's not always safe to approach a Crate Drop. Some gamers have their soldier hide near a Crate Drop and wait to ambush enemies as they approach them. This is a quick way to die, so always approach a Crate Drop with extreme caution.

Keep in mind that many inexperienced *PUBG* players are greedy as opposed to cautious. Thus, you can expect them to run toward a Crate Drop, for example, even if this means being out in the open. Doing this makes them easy targets. Use their inexperience, greed, and stupidity to your advantage, and get those easy kills when the opportunity presents itself.

Sometimes Crate Drops land in easy-to-access, wide-open areas. There are times, however, when they land in very difficult to reach locations.

YOUR INTERNET CONNECTION SPEED MATTERS!

When playing the PC or console version of *PUBG*, for example, if you have a slower Internet connection, you'll benefit from reducing the display resolution of the game from the Settings menu. To do this on a PC, from the Lobby screen, click on the gear-shaped Settings menu icon that's displayed in the top-right corner of the screen.

Highlight and select the Graphics submenu tab, and then adjust each option, based on the equipment you're using and the level of detail you want to see. If you know you have a slower Internet connection and/or a lower-end computer, you'll benefit from reducing the resolution and quality of the graphics generated by the game.

While the graphics won't look as awesome in a lower resolution, the speed of the game and your soldier's reaction time will improve slightly. If you have the game set at high resolution and you attempt to lie down in a grassy area, for example, thinking it'll provide camouflage and keep you out of your enemy's sights, you could be in for a bad surprise.

When your adversary has their resolution set lower, the detail of the grassy area won't be as detailed, and your soldier will sometimes appear as if they are simply lying on the ground, out in the open. Giving up more detailed graphics in favor of faster reaction time will often serve you well during a match.

When choosing your Region, select the one you're actually in to achieve the fastest connection to the game's servers. If you want to challenge yourself against players from a different region, you have the option of choosing an alternate region, but your connection to that *PUBG*'s servers will likely be slower.

SOUND PLAYS A CRUCIAL ROLE IN PUBG

The sound effects incorporated into *PUBG* play an important role in the game. Thus, it's a good idea to wear good quality headphones when playing. From the game's **Settings** menu, choose the **Audio** submenu and turn down the **Music** volume, but turn up the **Effects** and **UI** levels.

If you'll be playing Duo or Squad matches, you'll definitely want to use a gaming headset. This allows you to hear all of the sound effects, plus talk to your partner or squad mates in real time during each match. The importance of being able to communicate with your allies and coordinate well-planned attacks can't be emphasized enough.

Everything a soldier does in the game generates noise. The more noise your soldier makes, the easier it'll be for enemies to pinpoint their location and launch an attack. Footsteps from a soldier created while they're walking or running generate sound that intensifies the closer you are to them.

Opening and closing doors, using a weapon or item, and riding in a vehicle also generate noise that can be heard by enemies. Regardless of where you are or what you're doing, it's to your advantage to make the least amount of noise possible.

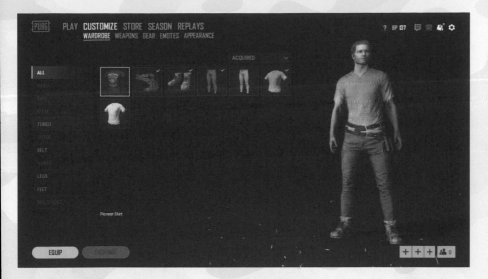

Prior to a match, take off your soldier's shoes. You'll be able to walk or run at the same speed as when your soldier is wearing shoes, but they will generate less noise when moving around. The difference in volume of footsteps when wearing shoes versus going barefoot has less of an impact now than it did in the past, but it's still something to consider if you want to travel around and potentially go unheard by your nearby enemies.

Keep in mind, soldiers generate different types of sound depending on the terrain they're in. Get to know the different types of sounds, so you can more easily identify where your enemies are located, what they're doing, and their distance from your soldier, simply by the noises they make.

PUBG has more than nine types of terrain, and when a soldier travels along each type of terrain, a different sound is created. Terrain types include: concrete, wood, metal, sand, carpet, stairs, grass, water, and paved roads. Remember, sounds will be louder the closer you are to your enemies. You'll also be able to tell, if you listen carefully, which direction the sounds are coming from, including if they're emanating from above or below you, so pay attention.

Some terrain sounds are very similar but being able to differentiate between them can help you determine from which direction an enemy is approaching, for example. Being able to identify sound effects clearly is one of the main reasons why you should play *PUBG* with quality headphones or a gaming headset.

MEMORIZE THE CONTROLS

Every action your soldier takes during a match is controlled using a game controller or a keyboard/mouse combination. Prior to a match, you're able to choose a game controller layout or customize your keyboard and mouse layout (key bindings). Once you make the customizations you deem necessary, memorize which button or key corresponds with each command or control.

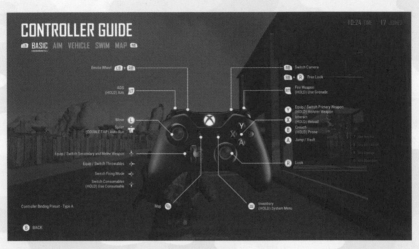

Keep in mind, if you're playing on a Windows PC, you have the option of using keyboard/ mouse controls or attaching an optional Xbox One controller to your computer system.

If you're using a console-based gaming system (an Xbox One or PlayStation 4), the default option is to use the game controller to control your soldier, but you always have the option of connecting a compatible keyboard and mouse to your console-based system.

PUBG Mobile takes advantage of the touchscreen on your smartphone or tablet to control the on-screen action. However, there are third-party controller options that can be used in conjunction with an iPhone, iPad, or Android-based mobile device. Shown here is *PUBG* Mobile (also known as *PUBGM*) on an iPhone Xs Max.

In addition to memorizing the main controls for moving your soldier around, as well as aiming, reloading, and firing your weapon(s), it's important to practice using the subtle motions your soldier is capable of, so you understand exactly how to jump, climb, crawl, swim, and use Health items. For example, you're able to free-look around your soldier. On a PC, this is done by holding down the ALT key while moving the mouse.

While aiming a weapon, have your soldier hold their breath when pulling the trigger to improve their accuracy. On a PC, this is done by holding the Shift key. Upon doing this, you'll be able to virtually zoom in slightly to your target, even without attaching an optional scope to your weapon. Keep in mind, your soldier can only hold their breath for so long. If they run out of air while aiming, it'll take several seconds to recover.

Another subtle, but useful action is to tip-toe, as opposed to walk. This causes your soldier to move slower, but it generates much less noise from footsteps. On a PC, for example, press the Ctrl key while walking to tiptoe instead.

Wasting even a fraction of second figuring out which button or key to press in order to complete an action during a battle could easily lead to your quick death.

If you're a *PUBG* newb, leave the controller or keyboard/mouse settings and key bindings at their default settings. Then, once you're more acquainted with the game, make customizations that could potentially improve your soldier's overall speed, reaction time, and aiming/shooting accuracy. Notice the option (displayed in the bottom-left corner of the screen) that allows you to return to the Default settings.

During a match, it's easy to switch between a first- and third-person viewing perspective. While using the third-person perspective, if you right-click the mouse (on a PC) while carrying a gun, this gives you a view looking down the sight of the weapon. Holding down the right mouse button switches to an over-the-shoulder view. Shown here is third person perspective (TPP).

Shown here is first person perspective (FPP).

While hiding behind a solid barrier and using it as a shield, one subtle move that can save your life by not making soldier's entire body visible and vulnerable is to lean out from behind the cover to see where your enemies are or to shoot, for example.

HERE'S WHAT IT TAKES TO SURVIVE

Survival during a match requires you to handle a wide range of tasks simultaneously, some of which include:

- Safely explore the island—including within all sorts of structures and buildings.
- Find and gather useful weapons, ammo, armor, and items.
- Maintain your soldier's Health, especially if he's injured from an attack.
- Avoid the Blue Wall and Red Zone.
- Travel around the island on foot or by driving a vehicle.
- Utilize the terrain surrounding your soldier to your advantage.
- Avoid ambushes and traps set by your enemies.
- Anticipate what your opponents will do, and quickly develop strategies to outsmart them.
- Attack and kill your adversaries.

Once you understand all of the components of *PUBG* and master how to use the weapons and tools at your soldier's disposal, if you want to ultimately win matches, you'll need to invest a lot of time practicing!

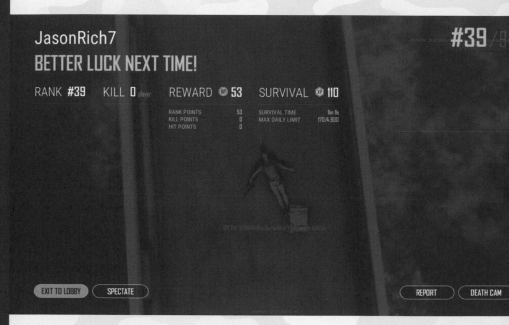

JasonRich7

BETTER LUCK NEXT TIME!

#39 /9

RANK **#39**   KILL **0** player   REWARD 🏅 **53**   SURVIVAL ⓍP **110**

RANK POINTS	53	SURVIVAL TIME	0m 0s
KILL POINTS	0	MAX DAILY LIMIT	170/4,800
HIT POINTS	0		

EXIT TO LOBBY   SPECTATE   REPORT   DEATH CAM

Each time you get killed, instead of immediately returning to the Lobby and entering into a new match, take advantage of Spectator mode. This allows you to watch the rest of the match you were just eliminated from. By watching other gamers, particularly in the final stages of a match, you can discover useful strategies and fighting techniques, plus get to know the island's terrain a bit better, while discovering where useful items are likely to be found during future matches. To enter into Spectator mode, from the Better Luck Next Time screen, choose the Spectate option that's displayed near the bottom-left corner of the screen.

After memorizing the controls, focus on developing your muscle memory (which takes plenty of repetition and practice), so you can focus your attention on developing strategies to kill off your opponents in the combat situations you're facing, as opposed to wasting time figuring out which keyboard/mouse or controller button to press.

This unofficial strategy guide is chock full of tips that'll help you become a better *PUBG* player and perform better in a wide range of combat situations. Realistically, nothing replaces the need to practice! Even once you know the secrets that'll help you become a better *PUBG* gamer, expect that you're going to be killed a lot more often than you're going to win matches. There's always going to be other players who are more experienced, who react faster than you, or who simply get lucky during a match.

Early on, instead of trying to win matches—and getting frustrated in the process—focus on staying alive within matches longer by fine-tuning your exploration and survival skills, while working to improve your kill count during each match. Keep your priorities straight as you progress through a match, without letting your emotions or taunts from your adversaries get the best of you.

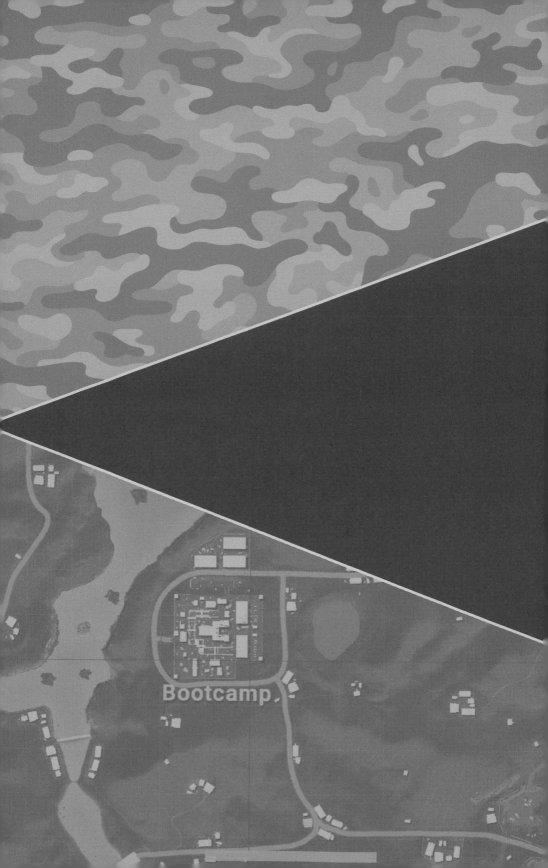

SECTION 2

CUSTOMIZING YOUR SOLDIER

ONCE YOU SET UP YOUR PUBG ACCOUNT AND LOAD THE GAME, YOU'LL BE ABLE to customize the appearance of your soldier.

WELCOME TO PLAYERUNKNOWN'S BATTLEGROUNDS

CREATE YOUR NICKNAME

Player nickname must start with a letter and may contain 4 to 16 characters with letters (a-z, A-Z), digits (0-9), dashes (-) and underscores (_)

JasonRich7 | CONFIRM

The first time you play *PUBG*, you'll be asked to create a nickname for yourself. This is the name that fellow gamers will see in conjunction with your soldier on the game screen. Your screenname must be unique.

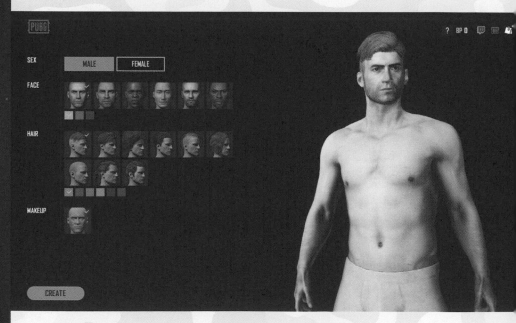

You're able to choose your soldier's gender (male or female).

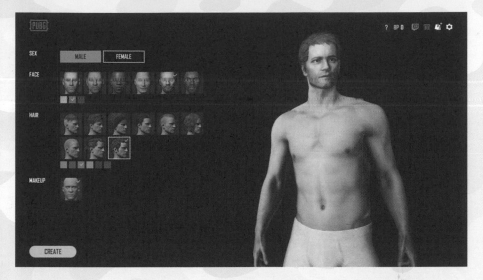

Next, customize your soldier's appearance. This includes choosing things like their skin color, their hair color and style, along with their makeup. As you play *PUBG*, you'll be able to purchase or unlock interesting makeup looks for both male and female soldiers.

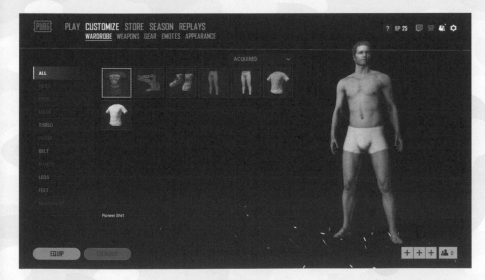

The first time you start playing *PUBG*, your soldier will be displayed in their underwear. You can start entering matches right away, although your soldier will be a bit underdressed. Built into the game are a collection of clothing items to choose from, including shirts/jackets, pants, hats, and shoes.

To display all of the currently available clothing options, select the ALL tab near the top-left margin of the screen. As you unlock or purchase more items, you can sort them by category, such as Head, Eyes, Mask, Torso, Outer, Belt, Hands, Legs, Feet, etc. Keep in mind, the selections you make are cosmetic only!

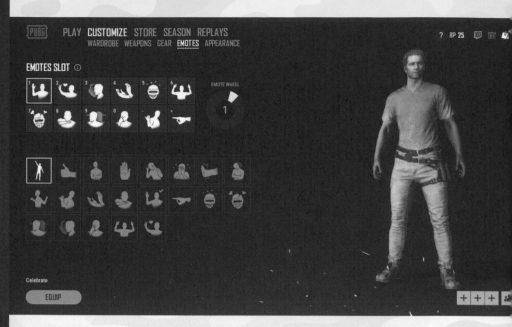

Part of the optional soldier customization process involves choosing from a selection of Emotes they will be able to showcase during matches. There are a dozen Emotes Slots to fill. In addition to the selection of Emotes that are unlocked right away, you'll be able to acquire more as you play *PUBG*.

During a match, access this Emotes menu to choose which emote you want to showcase at any time. All of the players with soldier's located near yours will see the gesture you opt to use. Some gamers use emotes to taunt their opponents, or to gloat after a kill. Others use them to communicate with teammates or squad mates who aren't using a gamer's headset and can't communicate using their voice.

Once you've invested a few minutes making your soldier look unique, save your changes and return to the Lobby screen. From here, you're able to choose your game play mode and enter into matches. At any later time (in between matches), feel free to revisit the Customize menu to alter your soldier's appearance.

As you participate in matches, you'll earn points that can be redeemed for more exclusive clothing and soldier customization items. You're also able to purchase clothing and appearance-related items from the game's online shop. Crates that are purchased (or unlocked by accomplishing in-game objectives) offer cosmetic clothing items used to customize your soldier's appearance.

Many different outfits, individual clothing items, make-up options, and limited edition sets of items can be purchased by accessing the Store option from the Lobby's Main menu. Notice that the limited-edition Joker Set can be purchased for $19.99 (US), but individual items from this set can also be purchased separately. For example, the Joker's Clothing can be purchased alone for $14.99 (US), and the Joker's Hair and the Joker's Makeup can be purchased separately for $5.00 (US) each.

As you're choosing what your soldier will look like, if you're an advanced player, you might want to avoid having your soldier wear items that require a lot of money or advanced skill to procure. Stick with basic outfit items. This way, your opponents will assume you're a newb and underestimate your fighting capabilities and experience during a match.

Crates, like this one, contained a selection of themed clothing items. Of course, you can pick and choose individual clothing items that come bundled with the game, that you've purchased, and that you've unlocked, in order to give your soldier a truly unique appearance.

One easy way to unlock more outfit items and emotes is to purchase a Survivor Pass. A Survivor Pass also allows you to participate in special missions, which if you're successful, result in additional items being unlocked. Each Survivor Pass is offered for a pre-determined time period before it's replaced with a new one at the start of each new *PUBG* gaming season.

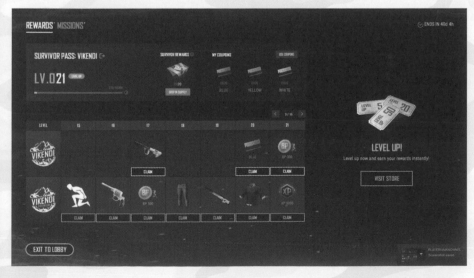

The main reason to acquire an optional Survivor's Pass is so you have the opportunity to participate in missions during your regular game play. When you successfully complete these missions, you'll unlock rewards.

It's also possible to purchase groups of Levels, which allow you to unlock mission-related prizes without actually having to complete the missions. Shown here, the ability to immediately unlock 20 Levels of the current Survivor Pass is about to be purchased for an additional $17.99 (US). This is in addition to the price paid for the Survivor Pass itself.

WAYS TO IMPROVE YOUR SOLDIER'S APPEARANCE

If you're a newb, avoid choosing bright-colored clothing items for your soldier. Bright colors are easier to spot in combat and make you stand out more on the island, which could put your soldier at greater risk. Camouflage or darker colored clothing tends to work best if you're looking to be as incognito as possible on the island.

While each Survivor Pass (also referred to as a gaming "season") is available, you'll have the ability to collect Coupons, which when you visit the Store and select the Coupon Shop option (shown here) allow you to acquire different and unique items that are typically not available elsewhere.

Remember, the cosmetic clothing items and customizations you make to your soldier's appearance do not impact their in-game capabilities or provide any advantages during combat whatsoever. New (optional) clothing and customization items are constantly being released.

Armor that you find and collect during a match does impact how much damage a soldier can withstand from an incoming attack. Seek out a Helmet (shown here) and Vest. Try to upgrade to a level 3 Helmet and Vest at the earliest opportunity during each match. Early in a match, you're more apt to find level 1 armor. Level 2 and level 3 are a bit harder to come across, but they provide better protection from attacks.

Once each match begins, you'll also want to find and grab a Backpack at your earliest convenience. Many Backpack designs are available. The design is for cosmetic purposes. What you need to focus on is the Backpack's level. This determines how much inventory your soldier can carry at once. Shown here is a level 1 Backpack about to be grabbed.

Other items, like Energy Drinks, can be found, collected, and then consumed when needed during a match to increase your soldier's Boost meter. Like other items, Energy Drinks take time to consume. You'll see the timer count down near the center of the screen as it's being used.

Finding and then using a First Aid Kit when your soldier's Health meter gets dangerously low allows you to replenish it and stay alive longer.

The fact that you can truly customize your soldier's appearance is one of the *PUBG* features that many gamers love. Sometimes, something as simple as adding a funny or unique hat (when not wearing a Helmet) will allow your soldier to showcase a unique personality. You can dress up your soldier so they look light-hearted and fun, or choose an appearance that's more menacing to strike some fear into your enemies (or at least intimidate them a bit).

How much time, effort, and money you invest into creating a unique appearance for your soldier is entirely up to you. Have fun and be creative with this aspect of *PUBG* or skip the Customization options and delve right into the Play option to start participating in matches.

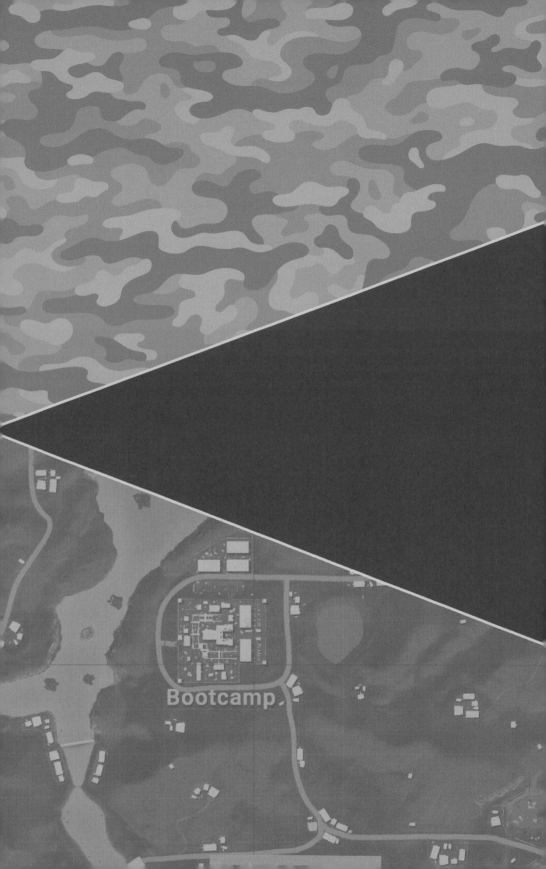

Bootcamp

DEVELOP YOUR SKILLS IN TRAINING MODE

From the Lobby screen of *PUBG*, highlight the Play option, and then from the submenu, choose the Training Mode option if you want to practice using the many different types of weapons, ammo, loot items, vehicles, and armor that are available during a normal match. As its name suggests, Training Mode offers a large area to practice your shooting techniques, without the risk of death.

Upon choosing Training Mode, it'll take several seconds for a group of additional gamers to join in, at which time, you'll be transferred to *PUBG*'s training area.

Unlike other gaming modes, you'll typically be joined by just a handful of other gamers (in this case 15), as opposed to up to 99 that would typically join a match. When in Training Mode, all of the same controls are available to you in terms of navigating within the game and controlling the movements and actions of your soldier.

Some of the more important control options (along with the keyboard, mouse, or controller buttons used to execute them) are displayed on the right margin of the game screen, above the mini-map. The location of this information will vary, however, based on which gaming system you're using. Shown here is the PC version of *PUBG* using a keyboard and mouse (an optional Xbox One controller is not connected).

Once your soldier is transported to the training area, the Match Starts In . . . countdown is displayed. When the counter reaches zero, you'll have 30 minutes per session to explore the training area and participate in the various training activities offered.

MASTER ESSENTIAL FIGHTING AND SHOOTING SKILLS

One of the first things you might opt to do once a training session begins is find and collect a Backpack. Within one of the larger buildings, you'll discover long tables with different types of armor, weapons, and ammo displayed on them. Choose a level 3 Backpack first so you can carry the maximum amount of inventory.

Next, grab some armor, including a Level 3 Vest and Helmet. While you won't need these armor items to survive within the training mode, it's good to get accustomed to wearing them and to experience firsthand the different types of damage each of these items can withstand before being rendered useless during an actual match.

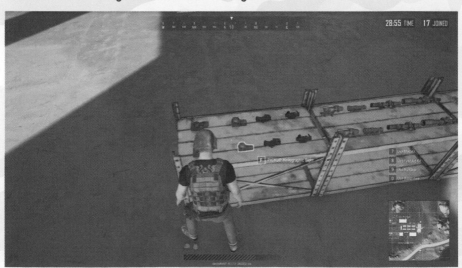

In addition to all of the different weapons available during matches, within Training Mode you'll also be able to try out each of the different weapon enhancements, including the Holographic Sight (shown here).

You'll also discover all of the different types of ammo that correspond with the various weapons. Grab what you need for the weapon(s) you've selected.

The training area is pretty massive. If you want to transport yourself around the area a bit faster, plus gain some experience driving a vehicle, look for a Scooter lying out in the open. Walk up to it. When prompted, press the Pick Up Scooter key or button to lift up the Scooter. Next, press the Get In Scooter button to mount it.

After hopping onto the Scooter, drive it around the training area. Just like during an actual match, other soldiers can shoot at you and the Scooter. While you won't die, the Scooter can be destroyed if it gets hit, so practice taking evasive maneuvers.

These large buildings contain stashes of weapons, ammo, weapon enhancements, and armor. Anything you discover lying on the tables and shelves is free to take and use. However, you can only pick up what you're able to carry within your soldier's inventory. Grabbing a level 3 Backpack will give you the most space to hold a variety of weapons, ammo, and related items.

Scattered throughout the training area are a selection of short-range and long-range shooting ranges. When you walk up to one of these shooting ranges, a selection of weapons and compatible ammo will be lying on the counters. Grab the weapon you want to use, collect some ammo, load (or reload) the weapon, and start shooting.

This long-range shooting range allows you to pick up different types of weapons and switch between them. If you have different types of Scopes or other compatible weapon enhancements within your Backpack, attach them to compatible weapons and practice using them as well.

Practice loading, reloading, aiming, and shooting each weapon on both still and moving targets. Visit the long-range shooting areas to practice hitting targets from a distance.

At any time, access your soldier's Inventory screen to learn more about the weapons, ammo, weapon enhancements, armor, and other items they are carrying. From this screen, select weapon enhancements and attach them to compatible weapons by dragging them from the column that displays what you're carrying to one of the weapons displayed on the right side of the screen.

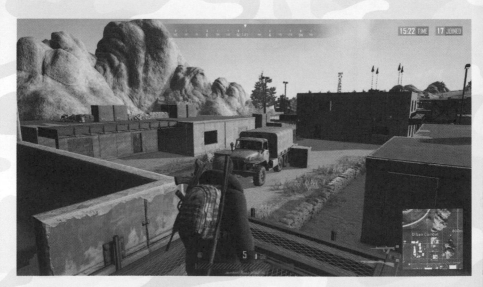

In addition to the long-range shooting ranges, Training Mode offers a variety of other areas that allow you to practice various shooting and maneuvering skills. Take the time to practice crouching, leaping over obstacles, climbing, using nearby objects for cover, and peeking around objects you're using for cover as you're simultaneously aiming and firing your selected and active weapon. These are all essential skills that'll come in handy during an actual match.

The large red and white banners displayed throughout the training area tell you about the different areas and activities available, and the types of weapons you can practice using in each area.

Another skill you'll need to master is the ability to climb through windows, shoot through windows, and hide behind objects for cover when you're being shot at (or hiding from enemies.) This obstacle course-like area allows you to practice some of these essential skills at your own pace.

Here, you can practice climbing, jumping up and down between levels, taking cover, and shooting from different heights, for example. Just as you would during actual matches, come up with creative ways to use your surroundings.

You'll discover several towers in the training area. Climb to the top of them and target any other soldiers you see moving around below. Being able to hit moving targets below you is another essential *PUBG* combat skill you'll want to perfect before engaging in actual matches.

At this close- and mid-range shooting area, the objective is to use your weapon to shoot at the green and red lights that spin around. Try switching between viewing perspectives and shooting modes so you get a feel for each weapon and the different ways each can be used.

This shooting range offers paper targets shaped like humans. Here you can practice shooting at close- and mid-range targets and test your aiming accuracy. Practice pulling the trigger multiple times in quick succession versus holding down the trigger to experience the recoil of each weapon and how each shooting option causes the vertical and horizontal recoil of a weapon to react differently.

Yes, you can shoot at other soldiers while anywhere in the training area. No, they won't get killed or be injured, but if they're wearing armor, direct hits will render the armor useless and it'll disappear once it's no longer of use due to excessive damage.

Especially if you can get other soldiers to cooperate, this obstacle course area offers a place to run around, climb, jump, hide, take cover, and practice shooting at moving enemies within a relatively confined space. These are skills that'll prove particularly useful during the end game portion of matches.

You don't need to spend an entire 30-minute period in Training Mode. At any time, you can exit out of Training mode (on a PC tap on the ESC key) to access a menu that offers a Leave Match option.

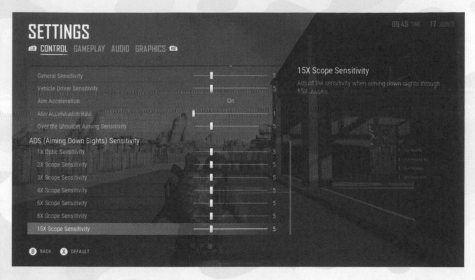

Press the ESC key (on a PC) to access this menu while in Training Mode. One listed menu option is used to access the game's separate Settings menu. Use this to access the Control, Gameplay, Audio, and Graphics submenus. From the Control submenu, try making small tweaks to the various settings, and then going back into Training Mode to see how each adjustment impacts the precision and control you have when moving your soldier around and using weapons, for example. Even a small change to the sensitivity of a submenu option can have a significant impact.

When you think you're ready, return to the Lobby, select the Play option, choose a game play mode, and enter into a match to put your combat skills to the ultimate life or death test.

OVERVIEW OF ITEMS

ASIDE FROM A VAST ASSORTMENT OF ARMOR, GUNS, WEAPON ENHANCEMENTS, and ammo, *PUBG* offers a selection of items that can be used in combat to help your soldier stay alive longer during a match. These items are used to boost your soldier's Health meter, enhance your soldier's speed, distract an enemy, or serve as a non-gun type of explosive weapon, for example.

ITEMS AVAILABLE ON THE ISLAND

While the selection of what's available to you during each match changes periodically as game updates are released, here's a summary of the more useful items that will likely be at your disposal during matches.

ITEM NAME	HOW IT'S USED	TIME IT TAKES TO USE
Med Kit	Replaces 100 percent of a soldier's Health meter. This item spawns randomly on the island (typically within buildings or structures), but is more often found within Crate Drops. Before using a Med Kit, make sure your soldier is somewhere safe, since they must remain still and not use a weapon during the time it takes for the Med Kit to work.	8 Seconds
First Aid Kit	Boosts a soldier's Health meter up to 75 percent. This item is a bit less common than Bandages, but it has a greater impact on Health with a single use. It's the perfect item to restore health after a battle that resulted in injury.	6 Seconds
Bandages	Replenishes a soldier's Health meter by 10, up to a maximum of 75 (out of 100). These are the most readily available items for boosting a soldier's Health meter. Multiple Bandages can be used in quick succession.	4 Seconds
Energy Drink	Increases a soldier's Boost meter by 40.	4 Seconds
Painkillers	Increases a soldier's Boost meter by 60.	6 Seconds

Adrenaline Syringe	Found mainly in Crate Drops and rarely as loot that can be found on the map, this item replenishes a soldier's Boost meter to 100 percent. This allows your soldier to run faster and replenish their Health faster, but only for a limited time.	6 Seconds
Gas Can	Quickly refill the gas tank of any drivable vehicle found on the island. The vehicle cannot be in motion when a Gas Can is used. To keep from becoming too vulnerable, it's best to gas up a vehicle before its tank runs dry. This allows you to choose where you'll stop to refuel, so you won't be a sitting duck out in the open.	3 Seconds
Cargo Drops	Also referred to as "Air Drops" or "Care Packages," these crates are dropped from aircrafts that fly overhead. Each crate contains a selection of powerful weapons, ammo, armor, weapon enhancements, and other useful items. You can often hear the turboprop airplanes flying overhead before the Cargo Drops are released, so pay attention. Once a Cargo Drop lands, it emits a cloud of red smoke, so it's easier to locate. As you'd expect, this smoke attracts attention from enemy soldiers, so approach with caution and watch out for snipers.	Not Applicable
Full Body Outfits	While clothing items can be mixed and matched to customize your soldier's appearance and armor can enhance their ability to withstand injury and damage, full body suits provide camouflage in different types of terrain. The Ghillie Suit is covered with leaves and blends in nicely with surrounding trees and bushes. The Woodland suit will help you stay hidden in forest and dense tree areas, while the Desert suit is ideal for staying out of sight in desert terrain. When visiting Vikendi, the Snow suit is white and will help keep you from being seen in snowy areas.	Not Applicable

Randomly scattered throughout the island, Bandages are typically found within buildings and structures. They can also be looted from soldiers that have been killed. When you find Bandages, pick them up and add them to your soldier's inventory until they're needed.

Energy Drinks can also be found and collected while exploring the island. Keep your eyes peeled as you're searching buildings and structures, because they're often found in piles of garbage, so they're difficult to spot until you're extremely close and looking down.

Gas Cans can often be found on the island in areas where there are no vehicles in the immediate area. If you anticipate needing to find and drive (or ride) a vehicle, grab a Gas Can so you can fuel up the vehicle as needed. However, if you don't plan to rely on a vehicle for transportation, storing unnecessary fuel in your soldier's inventory will take up valuable space.

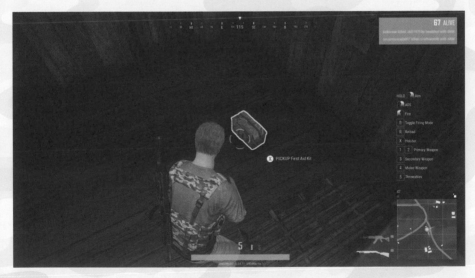

Because of their relatively large size, First Aid Kits are pretty easy to spot as you're searching buildings and structures. Anytime you find one, grab it and store it in your soldier's inventory until it's needed. Using a First Aid Kit to replenish your soldier's health in between firefights is a really good strategy, since you want to keep their Health meter as full as possible.

Using a Health or Boost-related item takes several seconds, during which time your soldier is vulnerable to attack. Hide behind a solid object, such as a wall, rock, or tree (shown here) to provide cover. The timer displayed in the center of the screen tells you how much longer your soldier needs to remain still for the item (in this case a First Aid Kit) to work. Do not move or attempt to use a weapon while the timer is ticking down or the item you're using will reset, and you'll need to start using it from scratch. This wastes valuable time.

Anytime you're using a Health or Boost-related item, a message will appear on the screen telling you which item is being used. This is not something your enemies see. However, if they know you've been injured, an enemy will suspect you'll use a Health replenishment item which will leave you vulnerable for a few seconds, so an experienced gamer will likely use this opportunity to attack.

While Bandages only boost your soldier's Health meter by 10, you can use multiple Bandages in quick succession to further replenish your soldier's health (up to 75 out of 100). The more Bandages you use, the longer it'll take, so make sure you're somewhere safe.

Using any type of Health-related item while out in the open is never a good idea, because you're fully vulnerable to attack. However, in this case (as you can see from the mini-map), this soldier is stranded in the island's unsafe area—on the wrong side of the blue wall. His only chance for survival is to keep boosting his Health meter which is quickly being run down. He also needs to keep moving, as fast as possible, toward the safe area in between using Health items.

Even by using all of his available Health boosters, including First Aid Kits and Bandages, this soldier was too deep in the unsafe zone and could not make it to safety before his Health meter was depleted. He died for a dumb reason, considering there were only 12 soldiers remaining alive on the island, and he had already managed to stay alive until the late stages of the match.

THROWABLE WEAPONS

Along with the many types of guns available on the island, there are several types of throwable weapons. Keep in mind, throwable weapons can bounce off solid walls and objects, so if you toss one and it bounces back toward your soldier, the resulting impact won't be pretty.

Throwable Weapon Type	What It's Best Used For
C4	This is an explosive hand grenade. Toss it toward enemies and the explosion will kill or injure them, depending on how close they are to the blast.
Frag Grenades	These too are explosive weapons that can be tossed. When detonated, the shrapnel flies all around and can injure or kill anyone in the blast zone.
Molotov Cocktails	These bottles are filled with explosive liquid. When tossed, a fire is created at the landing site. The fire can injure or kill enemies, depending on how close they are to the detonation and how much time they spend engulfed in flames. This is a great weapon for luring enemies out of their hiding places.

| Smoke Grenade | Toss one or more of these grenades to create a fast-forming cloud of smoke. This is best used to distract enemies and create a diversion when you're approaching to attack or need to retreat. |
| Stun Grenade | The boom from this weapon is designed to stun and shock enemies, making them temporarily immobile. This weapon has a blast radius of about 5 meters. A soldier caught in the blast will be blind and deaf for between 5 and 10 seconds. |

While hiding behind a wall, for example, you can use a throwable explosive weapon, such as a grenade, to weed out and injure (or kill) enemies lurking on the opposite site of the wall. When you're ready, leap up, toss your grenade, and then crouch back down behind the wall to avoid the blast. Once the grenade detonates, peek around the edge of the wall or over the top to see what damage you caused. If the enemy is drawn out into the open, be prepared to shoot'em dead with a gun.

This soldier appears to be trapped inside of a small building. By tossing Grenades and Smoke Bombs through the window, he hopes to create enough havoc so he can get out of the building safely. Notice that while the explosives are detonating, the soldier who threw them takes cover (in this case by crouching behind some crates).

Since the enemies are hiding outside behind a wall, the soldier in the building uses explosive grenades to lure them out into the open. At this point in the match, the safe area is very small and only 5 soldiers remain alive. Upon drawing out the enemy with throwable explosives, the soldier inside the building whips out a weapon and shoots at the enemy as he attempts to retreat to the left. In this case, the Grenade served its purpose and lured the enemy out into the open, as opposed to injuring him with the blast itself.

TYPES OF VEHICLES ON THE ISLAND

Many vehicles you'll discover on the island are broken down, rusted, or somewhat destroyed. These can be used to hide behind if you need temporary shielding, but they can't be driven. As you explore the island, there is a growing and ever-changing selection of vehicles that can, however, be driven. These will appear in good shape and when your soldier approaches one of them, you'll see a message near the center of the screen inviting your soldier to enter the vehicle so he/she can drive it or become a passenger.

Vehicles that have spawned on the island, but that have not yet been commandeered by an enemy will always be facing east. Even if another soldier has previously driven a vehicle, your soldier can still hop in and use it, but you'll often need to kill the original driver if he's still nearby (to ensure the vehicle has been left abandoned). You may also need to refill the vehicle's gas tank, using a Gas Can from your soldier's inventory.

If a vehicle's gas tank is empty, you'll need to use a Gas Can to refill it. These items can be found throughout the island and get stored within your soldier's inventory until they're needed.

The following is information about many of the types of vehicles that can be found on the island. Some are more useful when you're playing a Duo or Squad match, because they hold more than one soldier. Some also have multiple variants (meaning they look different but function the same way).

New vehicle types are periodically introduced into *PUBG* while others may be removed but could be re-introduced into the game at a later time.

VEHICLE TYPE	CAPACITY	MAXIMUM SPEED	USEFUL INFO
Buggy	2	90 to 100 km/hour	Due to its open frame, a Buggy does not offer too much shielding from incoming gun fire. It's a great all-terrain vehicle when it comes to speed and maneuverability.

(Continued on next page)

OVERVIEW OF ITEMS

UAZ	4	130 km/hour	This vehicle is rugged and provides good shielding, especially against small arms attacks. It's good for off-road driving. Some of the UAZ variants include a Soft Top, Hard Top, and Armored UAZ. The Hard Top and Armored models offer the maximum level of protection against incoming gunfire.
Dacia 1300	4	85 to 115 km/hour	This vehicle is not great for driving off-road, but on level roads it can reach a fast cruising speed. This vehicle is easy to disable if you shoot out more than one of its tires. You may find the horn built into this vehicle useful for summoning your partner or squad members, but you may get frustrated trying to get this vehicle to pick up enough speed to drive up a steep hill.
PG-117 Boat	5	90 km/hour	This is a fast-moving power boat that obviously can only be used in water. Its biggest drawback is the lack of a roof, so occupants are vulnerable to long-range weapon attacks from rifles with a scope.

| Motorcycle | 2 or 3 | Varies | This type of vehicle allows you to maneuver quickly and works well in a wide range of terrain types. Some of the Motorcycle variants include traditional two-wheeled motorcycles, motorcycles with a side car, Tuk Tuks (Tukshais), and Scooters. Motorcycles are great for performing tricks and mid-air stunts. |
| Jet Skis | 2 | Varies | These small water crafts are great for jetting through the water and being able to outrun enemy fire. They have a smaller turn radius than speed boats, so they're more maneuverable. |

This is a Motorbike with a Sidecar. It's harder to maneuver than a traditional Motorcycle, especially when it's carrying three passengers.

This Dune Buggy is ideal for off-road driving in the desert. It can climb hills, make sharp turns, and outrun many types of attacks. The drawback is that it's an open vehicle, so the driver or passengers can easily be killed by incoming gun fire.

Not all vehicles are ideal for all types of terrain. This multi-passenger van, for example, is having a bitch of a time trying to climb and maneuver around rough dirt terrain and steep hills. The progress is somewhat slow, but the van does provide some cover for its passengers from incoming gunfire.

The van has a much easier time driving along paved or flat roads and is able to achieve much faster speed on smooth terrain.

Other types of vehicles include multiple variants of trucks, sedans (passenger cars), a snow mobile (shown), and souped-up off-road vehicles. Each is capable of achieving different speeds, based on the terrain. Some offer better protection than others against bullets and explosive damage. Each vehicle handles differently (either in terms of speed or allowing its occupants to cross rough and hazardous terrain), and each works particularly well on specific types of terrain.

A sedan in the snow offers much less traction and speed than a snow mobile, for example. However, the sedan has a larger capacity if you're playing a Squad match, plus it's enclosed. This offers added protection from bullets.

As you're exploring, look for vehicles that'll help you in the situation you're in, and allow you to achieve your current objectives. For example, if you need to travel a great distance quickly, your vehicle choice will be different than if you need to climb steep mountains or cross rugged terrain and will need added protection from anticipated incoming attacks.

If you need to heal yourself, crouch or lie behind a car for cover, and then when your soldier's Health and/or Boost meter has been replenished, hop into the vehicle and drive toward your desired destination.

The Buggy is *PUBG*'s ultimate off-road vehicle, and probably the most fun to drive, especially on rough terrain. Practice making quick maneuvers and driving at the Buggy's top speed, since you'll need to outrun incoming attacks unless you have a passenger able to shoot back while you're driving.

Depending on the vehicle, some can be disabled or destroyed with direct hits from a gun. It's easier to damage or take out other vehicles using explosives. The tires on most vehicles are their most vulnerable area, so if you shoot and destroy two tires, this is typically enough to disable a vehicle.

VEHICLE DRIVING QUICK TIPS

The following tips will help you make the best use of vehicles while exploring the island:

- Just like real-life vehicles, in-game vehicles require gasoline to function. When a vehicle runs out of gas, it comes to an abrupt halt. Since there are no gas stations on the island, as you explore, it's important to find and collect Gas Cans which can be stored in your soldier's inventory until needed (but they do take up inventory space). If you plan to use a vehicle as a way to transport your soldier around the island, keep an eye on its gas gauge, so it does not run out of fuel at an inopportune time.

- One of the quickest ways to disable a vehicle being driven by an enemy is to shoot out several of its tires. (Most vehicles can still drive with one bad tire.) However, if you want to kill the enemy and commandeer the vehicle, shoot directly at the enemy and try to avoid damaging the vehicle.

- At the start of all matches, the vehicles that are drivable on the island all start off facing in an eastward direction. If you notice a vehicle is not pointed east, this means it's already been driven, and could be damaged or low on gas. The enemy who drove that vehicle previously could also still be nearby, waiting for you to approach the vehicle before killing you with an explosive grenade or sniper rifle, for example.

- If you're playing a Duo or Squad match, have one gamer drive a vehicle to distract your enemies and get their attention, while the second player approaches from a different direction (quietly on foot), and launches a surprise attack. Because vehicles make a lot of noise, they tend to attract a lot of attention.

- Anytime you're playing a Solo match and driving a vehicle, if someone starts shooting and you can't simply drive away quickly to avoid the incoming attack, exit your vehicle on the opposite side from where the bullets are coming from, and use your vehicle for cover. As the driver, you can't fire a weapon and drive at the same time, but you can maneuver the car into a position where it'll provide the best cover and protection once you exit the vehicle to shoot back at your attackers.

- Vehicles, including cars and motorcycles, are great for traveling across great distances quickly. However, they do take damage and act erratically when you fly over a cliff or make the vehicle go airborne, for example.

- A crashed vehicle can explode. If you drive over a cliff or directly into something and the vehicle explodes on impact while your soldier is still inside, you're toast!

- If you want to switch your active weapon, do this before

exiting the vehicle to save time and to utilize the vehicle for cover while you're still inside it.

- During the late stages of any match, you're better off getting around on foot and avoiding vehicles altogether, unless you're using one of them for shielding. When the safe zone is very small, traveling in a vehicle attracts a lot of attention and offers little or no advantage, since you typically have very small areas to travel across and the travel speed a vehicle offers won't be necessary.

- Anytime you need to hide behind a vehicle for shielding, and you don't plan to drive that vehicle again, shoot out its tires. Doing this will make the vehicle lower, so it provides more complete shielding. Otherwise an enemy could shoot under the car and potentially hit you. It's also possible to punch tires to destroy them, which makes less noise than a gunshot.

- Boats are used for traveling across bodies of water (across lakes or along rivers, for example) during a match. As long as a boat is traveling in a straight line while going a top speed, your soldier can jump out safely and land in the water. However, if the boat is turning even slightly while in motion and your soldier tries to jump out, they'll typically perish.

- Motorcycles are particularly versatile vehicles, because you can drive them across many types of terrain, up staircases, and even within buildings or larger structures. A buggy, however, can achieve maximum speed without using a Boost, while other vehicles cannot.

- Attempting to jump out of a moving vehicle is almost always deadly. Come to a full stop before leaving a vehicle.

- Just as you should never walk or run in a straight line when traveling on foot, when driving, don't drive in a straight line. Zigzag and go in an unpredictable pattern to make your vehicle an unpredictable moving target.

- In many vehicles, you need to be going at a decent speed in order to crash through certain objects. If you're going too slow, the vehicle will simply crash into the object (and get damaged or destroyed) instead of breaking it apart and going through it.

- Whenever you're playing a Duo or Squad match as you see multiple enemies riding in the same vehicle, aim to kill the driver, not the passengers. If you kill the driver first, the rest of the passengers will need to scramble a bit and become vulnerable, because they typically can't jump from a moving vehicle and survive.

SECTION 5

GET TO KNOW THE TERRAIN

PUBG HAS SEVERAL DIFFERENT ISLAND MAPS WHERE MATCHES TAKE PLACE. Each map is comprised of many points of interest, along with all sorts of locations worth exploring. Some locations that contain many buildings also contain a lot of powerful weapons, ammo, armor, and loot items to collect.

Other areas offer a good selection of decent weapons, ammo, armor, and loot items, while some areas of the island will offer lower quality or weaker weapons, ammo, armor, and loot. If you go online, you'll discover enhanced maps that outline the best places on the *PUBG* maps to collect the best and most powerful items.

Some of the independent websites to check out to see these interactive loot maps include:

- PUBGMap.io—www.pubgmap.io
- PUBGMap.com—www.pubgmap.com
- Gamepedia—https://pubg.gamepedia.com/Maps

For iOS mobile devices and available from the App Store, there's also the unofficial and free *PUBG Map* app. It will help you quickly find weapons, loot, and vehicles, regardless of which gaming system you're using. This is a free app that gets updated as new maps and content get added into the game itself. A similar app is available for Android mobile device from the Google Play Store. In the search field of either the App Store or Google Play store, type "PUBG Map" to find these apps.

Remember, buildings and structures located in remote areas of the island tend to have the worst collection of items or the weakest (level 1) armor and weapons.

GET TO KNOW THE PUBG MAPS

As of early 2019, *PUBG* offered four island maps—Erangel, Miramar, Sanhok, and Vikendi. PlayerUnknown periodically introduces new maps. Each map offers a collection of different locations and different types of terrain.

Erangel is approximately 8km by 8km in size and contains 51.47 percent land areas and 48.52 percent water areas. During a match on this island, more than 600 vehicles will typically be available, as will more than 24,000 loot spawns and 4,600 weapon spawns. Approximately 31 percent of the island is covered with dense foliage which can provide good cover.

Miramar is approximately 8km by 8km in size and contains 80.59 percent land areas and 19.41 percent water areas. During a match on this island, more than 450 vehicles will typically be available, as will more than 43,000 loot spawns and 7,900 weapon spawns. Approximately 33 percent of the island is covered with dense foliage which can be used for cover.

Sanhok is approximately 4km by 4km in size and contains 49.26 percent land areas and 50.74 percent water areas. During a match on this island, more than 195 vehicles will typically be available, as will more than 13,800 loot spawns and 4,500 weapon spawns. Approximately 43 percent of the island is covered with dense foliage which can be used for cover.

Vikendi is approximately 6km by 6km in size and contains 40.29 percent land areas and 59.71 percent water and ice areas. During a match on this island, more than 330 vehicles will typically be available, as will more than 28,600 loot spawns and 5,400 weapon spawns. Approximately 7 percent of the island is covered with dense foliage which can be used for cover.

One more advanced tactic is to reach a highly popular area upon landing that's far from the airplane's flight path. This often requires finding and utilizing a vehicle either to reach that location upon landing, or to escape that location and reach the safe area of the island once the blue wall forms and the island's safe area starts to shrink. This technique allows you to quickly collect higher-end weapons and armor, while potentially encountering fewer enemies early in the match.

As each match progresses, the amount of damage your soldier receives as a result of being on the wrong side of the blue wall (outside of the safe circle) will increase, as will the speed at which your soldier's Health meter gets diminished. While you're working toward becoming a better *PUBG* gamer, it's a good idea to stay within the safe circle. Once you get more acquainted with the game, you can venture into the unsafe zone for small amounts of time, as needed, to launch an attack or retrieve valuable items.

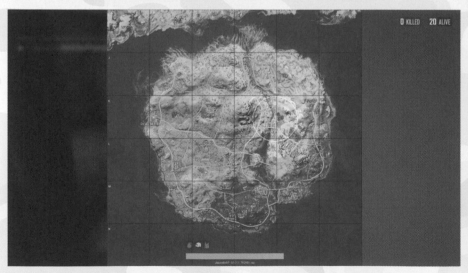

Each time a new circle appears on the map, indicating exactly where the blue wall will be shrinking around next, immediately start heading toward the next safe zone, keeping in mind that enemies will also be traveling toward the safe zone at the same time. You'll likely encounter one or more of them, especially toward the later stages of a match, when the safe area of the island becomes very small.

As you move into what will be the next safe zone during a match, don't immediately head toward the center of that zone. If you do, you'll often get surrounded by enemy soldiers and have to fight them off from multiple directions at once.

You're better off keeping your back to the blue wall and staying near the edge of the safe zone, so you can put more emphasis on what's happening in front of your soldier, as well as to the sides.

On the map screen, the yellow dot indicates your current position in Solo mode. If you're playing a Duo or Squad match, each soldier on your team is depicted with a different colored icon. You're never able to see the location of your enemies on the map.

Each *PUBG* map offers many distinct locations. Memorizing the layout of each location can be a time-consuming process that requires firsthand exploration, not just studying the map screen. To enhance your gaming experience as you're becoming acquainted with new maps, get to know one area of the map at a time, and stay within the known areas as much as possible.

Understanding the terrain allows you to focus on other elements of the game, without wasting time having to switch to the map screen often. Instead, you'll be able to stick with the mini-map, yet still be able to navigate around efficiently and safely.

One way to save some time, instead of switching between the game screen and the map screen while aboard the aircraft is to mark your desired landing location on the map while you're still in the pre-deployment area. Here, location markers are displayed in different colors. Each represents the desired landing position of a particular squad member. The key that shows which player goes with each colored marker is seen in the bottom-left corner of the screen.

As your soldier is freefalling or parachuting toward land, look all around your soldier and take note of any enemies that will be landing close by. Ideally, you want to land near structures that remain deserted, so you can collect the weapons and ammo inside before encountering enemies.

HOW TO COLLECT AND MANAGE YOUR SOLDIER'S ARSENAL

AT ANY GIVEN TIME, YOUR SOLDIER CAN HAVE A PRIMARY AND SECONDARY weapon that's easily and quickly accessible, but they can also hold up to three additional weapons. Switching between weapons that are not your primary and secondary weapon takes slightly longer.

KEY GUIDE
DEFAULT SETTINGS

When using a keyboard/mouse combo to control your soldier in *PUBG*, be sure to memorize all the key and button options for managing and controlling your soldier's weapons.

If you're using a keyboard/mouse combo to control your soldier on a PC, by default, the "5" key allows you to select the grenade weapon and then toss grenades that you've collected and that have been added to your arsenal. When your soldier has multiple types of grenades, press the "5" key repeatedly to toggle between them.

Make sure you remember which type of weapon is stored in each inventory slot, so you can quickly access the right weapon at the right time without having to guess or scroll through all of the weapons you're holding.

You may think a Crossbow is a weak and useless weapon, but with practice, you can achieve kills (even from a distance) with a single headshot, regardless of whether or not the enemy is wearing a Helmet. Take advantage of Training Mode to practice using this and other weapons before needing to use them during a match. The Crossbow is also a silent weapon, so it can be used when you don't want nearby enemies to hear your gunfire.

CHOOSE THE BEST FIRING MODE FOR EACH GUN

Almost every weapon allows you to manually switch between Single Shot, Burst, or Automatic firing mode. Which you choose is a matter of personal preference. Use the Toggle Fire Mode controller button or keyboard key to switch between firing modes, when applicable, based on the weapon your soldier is currently holding.

- **Single Shot** mode shoots one bullet a time, each time you press and release a gun's trigger.
- **Burst** mode shoots two or three bullets at a time, each time the trigger button is pressed on most types of guns.
- **Automatic** firing mode activates when the trigger button/key is held down. It keeps shooting bullets from the gun until it runs out of ammo. When using Automatic mode, the longer you hold down the trigger, the worse the weapon's aim will become, as the horizontal and vertical recoil will intensify. Some of this recoil can be counteracted using weapon enhancements.

START LOOTING ONCE YOU LAND

Starting immediately upon landing on the island, start the looting process by seeking out and grabbing weapons, ammo, armor, and other items that you'll need to engage in combat and survive during your stay on the island.

Anytime you're looting on the island, which means you're collecting weapons and items, use the "Tab Grab" method to speed up the process when it comes to picking up multiple items at once. Use the Interact controller button or keyboard key if you just need to pick up one item at a time. Tab Grab (on a PC) allows you to pick up all items that are close together with a single action, as opposed to grabbing one item at a time, which takes longer.

Your first objective once your soldier lands on the island should be to find and grab a gun, along with compatible ammo. Don't waste time grabbing other items until you're armed and can protect yourself. During this initial looting process, run around as fast as you can (especially if there are enemies in the vicinity), and be sure to explore buildings and structures carefully looking for good stuff to collect.

As soon as your soldier picks up a gun, immediately load it with compatible ammo, so you're ready to shoot. Never walk around with an unloaded gun. If you wait until you need to fight before loading (or reloading) your gun, you'll waste valuable time when you're being confronted by one or more enemies. You could wind up dead while waiting for your weapon to load.

There are many types of guns to find and collect on the island. Each has a compatible type of ammunition, and most have extra weapon enhancements that can be attached to the weapon to improve its shooting accuracy, the number of bullets it holds, or its response time. From the Inventory screen, learn about the weapons, ammo, and items your soldier has collected and that are available in the nearby area.

PUBG offers six main categories of guns, including Assault Rifles (ARs), Submachine Guns (SMGs), Shotguns, Sniper Rifles, Pistols, and Light Machine Guns (LMGs). Each weapon has its own capabilities, making it more useful in specific types of combat situations.

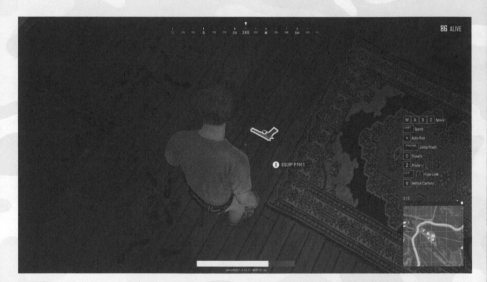

Pistols are a close-range type of weapon. Because they're the least powerful of the guns, they tend to be more useful at the start of a match, but much less useful as a match progresses.

Within each gun category, there are several distinct gun types available, although most (but not all) guns within a specific category will use the same type of ammo. It's important to learn which ammo type goes with each gun. For example, Shotguns use 12-gauge shells.

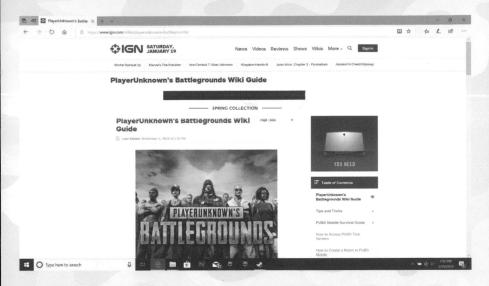

Because new guns and weapons are continuously being added to *PUBG*, visit a website, such as IGN's PlayerUnknown's Battlegrounds Wiki Guide (www.ign.com/wikis/playerunknowns-battlegrounds), to discover the most current selection of guns, and the type of ammo that's used with each.

Each type of gun is best used from a certain range. Some, like Pistols, are close-range weapons. Others are better suited for mid-range combat, or when your enemies are far away. Sniper Rifles, for example, are ideal for picking off enemies from an extreme distance, especially when a powerful Scope enhancement is added to the Sniper Rifle.

After grabbing a gun, access your soldier's Inventory screen and select that weapon to learn about its Power, Effective Range, Stability, and Firing Rate, along with the type of ammo it uses and how much ammo it can hold.

In addition to paying attention to a gun's range, acquaint yourself with how many bullets or rounds it can hold. This determines how often you'll need to reload. How much time it takes to reload varies greatly based on the type of weapon your using. Some guns have a quick reload time, but only hold a few rounds of ammo at once, while others hold many rounds of ammo, but take longer to reload. All of this gun-related information matters when you're engaged in an intense and time-sensitive combat situation.

When you point a gun (without a Scope) at an enemy, its targeting sight will be displayed. The size of the crosshairs you see matters a lot. The smaller the crosshair, the more accurate your aim will be. For example, if your soldier is in motion while shooting, the crosshair will be large, and the gun's accuracy will be lower.

Having your soldier stand still and/or crouch down will improve their aim, as will having them hold their breath while aiming the gun.

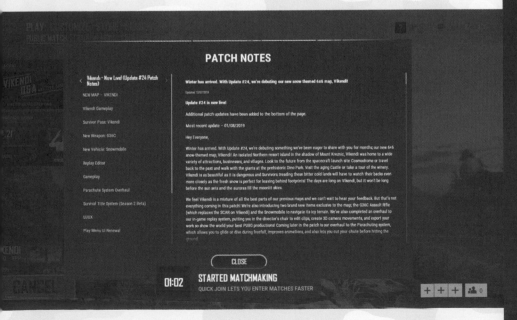

Landing a headshot when shooting at an enemy always causes the most damage. If your enemy is wearing no Helmet or a low-level Helmet, a single headshot will often kill your enemy. If they are wearing a level 3 Helmet, it can often withstand one or two direct bullet hits, but how much damage you inflict will depend on the type of gun/ammo you're using, the accuracy of your aim, and your distance from the enemy.

Whenever new weapons arc introduced into *PUBG*, they're described within the Patch Notes. You can access the latest Patch Notes from the Lobby screen by clicking on the icon that's displayed near the top-right corner (PC version). Once you learn about a new weapon, be sure to test it out firsthand within Training Mode so you get a feel for it before you need to use it during a life or death battle that take place during a match.

DISCOVER THE BEST WEAPON ENHANCEMENTS (ATTACHMENTS)

As important as it is to find and collect the most powerful weapons as you're exploring the island and preparing for combat, it's equally important (especially once you reach beyond the midpoint of a match) to equip your most powerful weapons with weapon enhancements.

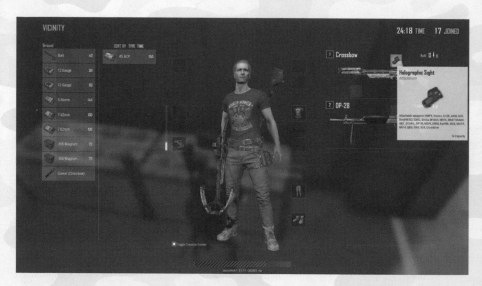

Weapon enhancements, like the Holographic Sight (shown here), can be found on the island and collected within your inventory. However, from your soldier's Inventory screen it's necessary to manually connect a weapon enhancement to a compatible weapon in order to make use of it.

Muzzle Attachments are one type of weapon enhancement. For pump and double-barrel shotguns, a muzzle attachment is called a Choke. This keeps the bullet fragments (pellets) from each shot from spreading out too much, so each shot focuses in on a smaller target area, thus causing more damage.

Assault Rifles, Sniper Rifles, and SMGs, for example, can use a Compensator. This controls the weapon's recoil and helps you maintain more accurate aim when taking multiple shots in quick succession.

Flash Hiders work with specific types of weapons and when attached to a gun that's being shot, hides its muzzle flash. This makes it harder for your enemy to visually see where an attack is coming from. However, using their ears, they can often hear which direction bullets are approaching from.

Flash Hiders work great with Sniper Rifles and Assault Rifles being used from a distance from your opponent. When you're hiding in a bush or using some other type of cover, and don't want your enemies to be able to determine the exact location where you're perched and shooting from, a Flash Hider is useful. It can also reduce the weapon's recoil.

In general, you always want to have a compatible muzzle weapon enhancement attached to the gun you're using. One of the more popular types of muzzle is a Suppressor. Many types of guns have Suppressors available for them. It both hides the flash from the gun when it's shot and serves to reduce the weapon's recoil. Reducing recoil improves shooting accuracy.

In many cases, the Suppressor also eliminates the "bang" (the firing sound and the bullet echo) heard from each shot, which makes it that much harder for an enemy to figure out where you're shooting from if you're not in their direct line of sight.

Grips (also known as Under Barrel Attachments) reduce horizontal and/or vertical recoil, depending on the type of Grip that's attached to the compatible weapon.

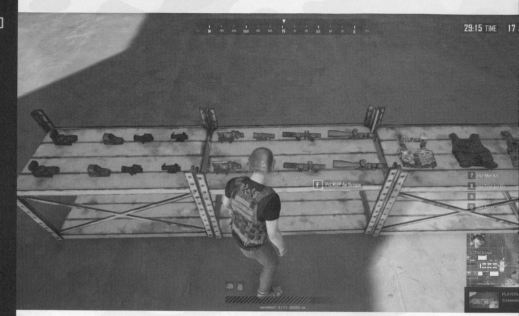

PUBG offers many different types of Scopes (also referred to as Sights) that can be attached to compatible weapons. A Sight allows you to zoom in on your enemy and see them from far away, thus increasing the shooting accuracy of long-distance shots. Practice using each type of Sight within Training Mode (shown here).

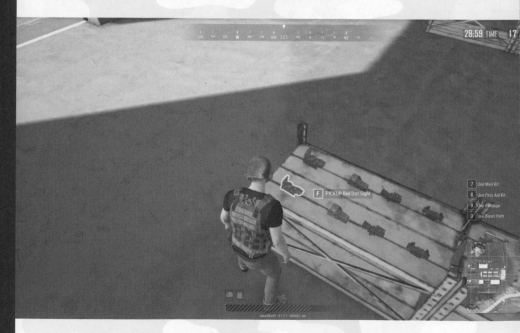

In addition to various scope magnifications, there are different types of Sights that allow you to see different details when looking through the Scope. Not all Scopes work with all guns, however. Some of the standard types of Scopes available include a Holographic Sight and a Red Dot Sight (shown here).

You'll also discover Scopes that improve your ability to zoom in on your enemies from a distance. There's a 2x magnification Scope, as well as a 4x magnification Scope (which is the most versatile when at mid- or long-range from your enemy). The 8x Scope is ideal for single shot Assault Rifles as well as many types of Sniper Rifles.

When you're very far away from an enemy and using an 8x Scope, for example, you will experience some bullet drop. This means that the bullet will land a bit lower than where you aim in your Sight, so it's important to compensate for this based on the weapon you're using and the distance you are from your enemy.

One of the "crate only" Scopes is a 15x magnification. This means you can only obtain this type of powerful Scope by discovering it within a crate or by killing an enemy that's carrying one. This is the Scope you'll use for taking extremely long-range shots that require superior accuracy. It's the least versatile of the Scopes, however.

During the late stages of a match, the more powerful Scopes are much less useful, because as the circle shrinks, you and your enemies are forced closer and closer together, so there's little need for a long-range weapon.

As you prepare for the late stages of a match, make sure you have a lower-intensity Scope, such as a red dot, 2x, or 4x Scope at your disposal. This will be more useful than an 8x or 15x Scope.

Yet another type of weapon enhancement available within *PUBG* are called Stocks. This weapon add-on helps to improve its accuracy and stability. Bullet Loops, which are a type of Stock, are used to shorten a compatible gun's reload time.

Magazines (also called Mags) are used to store and use more bullets within a gun without needing to reload. There are several types of Magazines, some of which also speed up a gun's reload time.

PUBG OFFERS THREE AIMING MODES

It's important to understand that when it comes to shooting, *PUBG* has three different aim modes.

The first aiming mode is referred to as "hip firing." This is done by shooting the weapon without simultaneously pressing the Aim button on the controller or keyboard.

With most guns that are able to shoot multiple shots in quick succession, the recoil increasingly reduces the aim accuracy of the weapon. For this reason, it's often better to keep tapping the trigger to shoot individual shots quickly than it is to hold down the trigger button for continuous fire with compatible guns.

The benefit to using hip fire mode to shoot is that your soldier can simultaneously run and shoot at the same time. Using the other two shooting modes requires your soldier to stand still or just walk while using them. Many experienced *PUBG* players often use the hip fire mode anytime they're using a shotgun, because with this type of gun, the accuracy barely changes if you switch to a different shooting mode.

Hip firing is the least accurate, especially if you're shooting an enemy from mid-range or from a great distance.

Holding down the Aim button while shooting allows your soldier to use the game's second shooting mode. When using the first-person viewing perspective, the crosshair from the weapon decreases in size, and the resulting horizontal recoil is greatly reduced, especially if you're shooting multiple shots in quick succession.

Holding down the Aim button while shooting can be used anytime you're using a Pistol, but it works nicely with most other guns as well, because it allows your soldier to aim the gun more precisely and achieve greater target accuracy.

Anytime you're holding down the Aim button and attempting to fire a shot, your soldier will need to stand still (for greater accuracy) or walk. It's not possible to run and shoot at the same time. With many types of guns, this shooting mode works well with mid-range shots, but can also be used with distance shots, but the recoil and accuracy will vary based on the weapon being used.

Aim Down Sight (ADS) is the third shooting mode that *PUBG* offers. You'll quickly discover this shooting mode offers the best accuracy with most types of guns, because ADS greatly reduce horizonal and vertical recoil while shooting. If your goal is to knock off players with single bullet headshots (which takes practice), you'll need to master using the ADS shooting mode.

When using ADS, make your soldier hold his/her breath—this increases shooting accuracy even more. This strategy is a great alternative early in a match if you haven't yet found and attached a powerful Scope to your weapon and you want to take mid-range or distance shots without wasting a lot of ammo.

While using ADS, your soldier is also able to lean. This is a movement that comes in very handy when you need to peek around corners or around an object your soldier is hiding behind. By leaning, less of your soldier's body gets exposed, but you're still able to see around various objects.

During most combat situations, regardless of the type of gun you're using, ADS should be your default shooting mode, although you'll want to invest time practicing with it and various types of weapons before entering into combat. One situation when ADS is not ideal is if your enemy is very close to you. In this case, don't waste the fraction of a second it takes to switch to ADS mode, just aim and shoot.

PEEKING CAN HELP YOU SURVIVE IN COMBAT

Peeking allows you to pop your head out from behind an object and see what's out there (or around a bend, for example), without exposing too much of your soldier's body. Leaning right or leaning left is one method of peeking.

If you're standing behind a narrow object, one useful strategy is to randomly peek right and shoot, and then peek left and shoot at your enemy. This makes it harder for your opponent to shoot back, because they don't have time to properly aim, since they don't know which side of the object your soldier will peek out from.

Another way to confuse your enemy a bit using Peek is to crouch down when peeking left or right. The result is your soldier will be lower down than your enemy might expect, so if they're aiming for a head shot and they expect your soldier to be standing, their aim will be too high. Consider randomly peeking left and right while standing, and randomly crouch down while peeking as well to avoid being shot at, yet still get to see, aim at, and shoot your nearby enemies while taking cover behind an object and not overexposing your soldier's body.

KEEP YOUR ENEMIES GUESSING

Always try to make your enemy guess about what you'll do next. Avoid patterns in your movement or actions and be as random as possible when using peek or moving across an open area, for example.

If you're hiding behind an object, peek out and shoot at an enemy but miss the shot, instead of staying behind the same object, try moving a bit to get a different vantage point, hide behind something else, and then peek out and shoot from there. Again, this will make your soldier harder to track and aim at. Anytime you get repetitive with your strategies or actions, this makes it that much easier for enemies to predict what you'll do next, prepare, and then attack accordingly.

Anytime an enemy can guess where you're going or what you're about to do, this places you at a huge disadvantage, so be spontaneous! Force an enemy to have to react to your seemingly random actions—not the other way around.

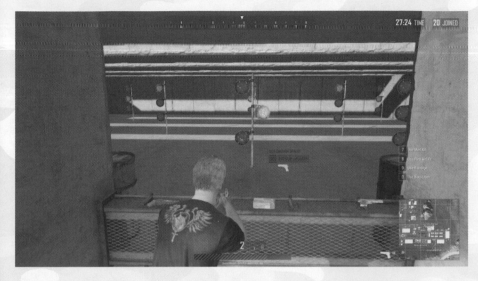

The best way to improve your aim when using the various weapons is to spend time experiencing *PUBG*'s Training Mode. In addition to seeing how each weapon works firsthand, practice using each weapon while standing still, peeking out from behind an object, crouching, walking, and, if applicable, while running.

Whenever possible, get to the high ground! You're almost always better off being higher up than the enemy you're shooting at. For example, climb to the top of a hill or mountain. Shoot at enemies from the roof of a building, or from the top of a staircase. A height advantage will usually work in your favor. Also, if you need to climb a hill on foot, jumping while running will speed up your travel time.

Try to avoid crossing a wide open and vast area, including when you need to enter into water. This makes you an easy target. Whenever possible, try to find an alternate route that provides some cover while getting you to your desired destination. Newbs will often try to cross open areas, so watch out for them so you can achieve easy kills.

Anytime you're shooting at moving enemies that are off in the distance, allow for bullet travel time. This is the small amount of time it takes for bullets to leave your gun and reach their target. If your enemy is in motion, aim just slightly ahead of them, to compensate for bullet travel time.

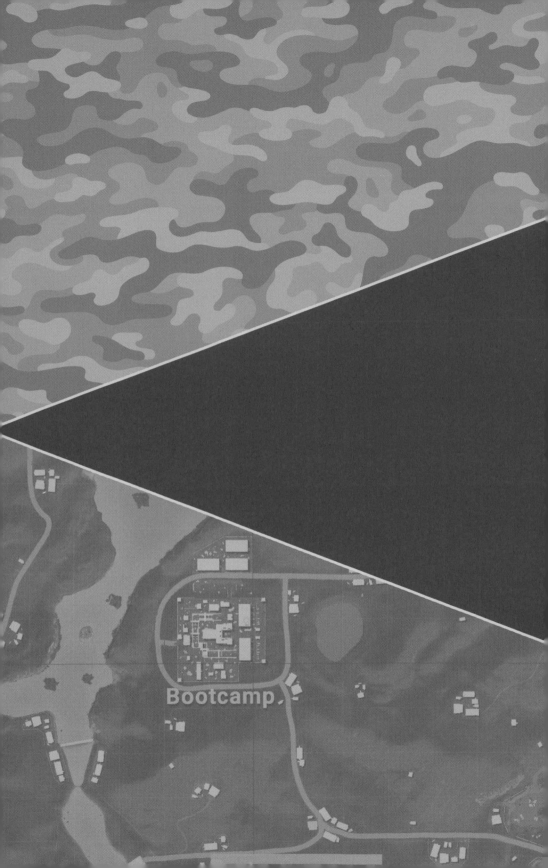

COMBAT TECHNIQUES THAT'LL KEEP YOU ALIVE

YOU ALREADY KNOW THAT YOUR SOLDIER HAS A HEALTH METER. EACH TIME your soldier gets injured as a result of a fall, being too close to an explosion, or by getting hit by a bullet, for example, some (or in some cases all) of their Health gets depleted.

KEEP YOUR SOLDIER HEALTHY DURING EACH MATCH

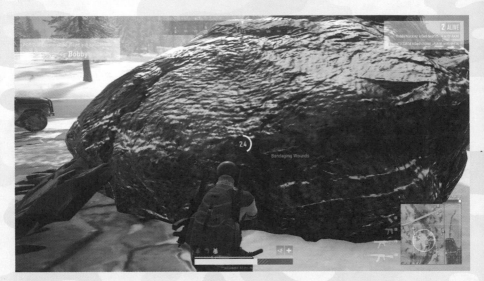

As long as your soldier has at least some health remaining, they can be healed using First Aid Kits, Med Kits, and Bandages (shown here).

First Aid Kits and Bandages can only heal your soldier up to the 75 percent mark on their Health meter.

Bandages take 4 seconds to use, during which time your soldier is vulnerable to attack, so make sure you're in a safe spot before using this item. Bandages each boost your Health meter by 10 points.

First Aid Kits require 7 seconds to work, during which time your soldier is vulnerable to attack and can't shoot a weapon or move around. Regardless of what level your Health meter is at, when used, a First Aid Kit will replenish it to 75 percent.

If your Health meter is already above 75 percent, don't bother using a First Aid Kit, as it'll do nothing for you.

Med Kits require 10 full seconds to work, during which time your soldier can't move or use a weapon. The benefit of a Med Kit is that it replenishes your soldier's Health meter to 100 percent, regardless of where it was previously.

After every fighting situation, take a few moments to heal your soldier and replenish their Health meter before you're forced to engage in another firefight. It's always better to enter into a battle with a full Health meter, so your soldier can withstand a greater amount of damage before getting killed. Be sure to take cover when you need to heal your soldier.

Yes, you have to stay still while a Med Kit or First Aid Kit, is working. However, you can start moving again when the counter reaches 0.5 seconds. You don't have to wait that extra half-second to begin moving again. If you move too soon, however, you'll have to start using that item again from scratch and the timer will reset.

Energy Drinks and Pain Killers (also referred to as Boosters) are items that can be collected, stored within a soldier's inventory, and then used (as needed) to increase a soldier's Boost Bar. When at least three sections of the Boost Bar (displayed immediately above the Health Bar) are full, this will allow your soldier to temporarily run faster and heal faster when your soldier takes damage (gets knocked). Gamers often refer to getting injured as getting "knocked" when playing *PUBG*.

SURVIVAL TIPS THAT'LL HELP YOU STAY ALIVE LONGER

One of the biggest perks of playing a Duos or Squad match is that in addition to working together to launch coordinated attacks, one team member is able to revive another who gets injured. Simply approach the injured soldier and press the Revive button on your controller or keyboard. It takes 10 seconds to revive a team mate.

When reviving a soldier or being revived, both soldiers need to remain still and cannot use a weapon to defend themselves. Before moving in to heal an ally, make sure it's safe to do so, or you and your team mate or squad mate could both wind up dead from a single enemy attack. Knowing this, watch for when your enemies are reviving each other. This represents the perfect time to launch your own attack.

By studying the island map and developing an understanding of the terrain you're in, you'll discover the best locations to hide, the most useful places from which to launch attacks, as well as locate where you're most likely to discover weapons, ammo, armor, and useful items. As you're first exploring each of the island maps, invest as much time as you can learning the nuances of the terrain. By doing this, you'll initially wind up getting killed more often than not, but as you play more and more matches on that island, you'll discover the terrain knowledge you develop will prove to be extremely useful in the future.

Remember, during the early stages of a match is when you want to collect weapons, ammo, armor, and loot items. As the match progresses, always be trying to upgrade your weapons and armor (as well as your Backpack). Unless you're forced into combat earlier, try to wait until midway through the match at the earliest, before you start fighting and launching attacks.

Anytime you enter into a new building or structure, first clear it out by killing your enemies or chasing them out of the area before you change your focus and start looting the place. If you don't see enemies right away, listen carefully for the sounds they make. Keep in mind, an enemy could hide within a room, close the door behind them and then wait for you to enter in order to launch a surprise attack. Be ready for this anytime you enter into a new room where you suspect an enemy might be lurking. (Of course, you can also have your soldier hide in a room, behind a closed door, and wait to attack an enemy who enters.) As always, the element of surprise will serve you well.

Sometimes, the best survival approach is simply to hide and have your soldier remain motionless and very quiet. Let as many of the remaining enemies kill each other off. This is referred to as "tactical camping."

Battles can sometimes extend on for a while, so it's best to engage in fights while well inside the safe zone. If you're up against the edge of the safe zone and the blue wall starts to move, you'll then have to move to the safe zone during a battle. Getting shot at by an enemy and getting caught on the wrong side of the blue wall at the same time is a recipe for disaster.

Anytime you know one or more enemies are hiding out behind an object in an otherwise open area, consider tossing a few explosive grenades at those enemies to inflict injury and lure them out into the open. As soon as you toss the grenades, switch to a loaded gun. As soon as the enemies show themselves, quickly shoot'em dead.

Grenades are also useful when you're rushing an area where you know an enemy is hiding. As you're running toward the location (especially if you're out in the open), toss a few grenades to cause some disruptive and distracting explosions, and then quickly switch to a gun as you get closer, so you're able to shoot at the enemies that are hopefully a bit surprised and disoriented from the preceding explosive blasts.

If you know the safe zone is about to shrink and you injure but do not kill an enemy, it sometimes makes sense to leave the immobilized enemy to die from exposure to the blue wall, as opposed to going in for the kill yourself. Whether or not you go in for a kill should depend on how safe you feel doing so, based on everything else currently happening in the match.

This also applies if you've killed your enemy and need to decide whether or not to approach the corpse to collect what the deceased enemy has left behind, or instead, do what's necessary to ensure that you're able to get your own soldier to safety.

Anytime you're hiding out in any type of building or structure, take a moment to figure out multiple escape routes, aside from exiting through the front door. Determine if there are alternate doors or windows you can quickly escape through, if enemies attempt to rush and breach the structure you're occupying. Especially if you're playing a Duos or Squad match, or you're in a well-populated area, it's easy to become trapped within a building. Unless you have appropriate weapons and an ample supply of ammo, as well as the combat skill needed, fighting your way out of a building, especially when the perimeter is being guarded, can be tricky.

Smoke Grenades don't cause any damage to an enemy, but they're really useful for causing distractions and diverting your enemy's attention. The smoke can also block an enemy's view as you make an escape, for example. Remember, the smoke only covers a small area and then dissipates rather quickly.

If you need to create a distraction, toss a Smoke Grenade as far as you can in one direction, wait for it to detonate, and then run in the opposite direction—away from the smoke. The smoke will likely attract enemy attention away from your actual location and the direction you're intending to travel.

THIRTY PROVEN SURVIVAL STRATEGIES

THE FOLLOWING ARE A COLLECTION OF PROVEN PUBG STRATEGIES THAT'LL help you boost your successful kills, plus survive longer during each match.

#1—GRAB ANY WEAPON QUICKLY

As soon as you land on the island, quickly grab any weapon and compatible ammo, load that weapon, and get ready to fight! This will increase your chances of surviving the early stages of a match. If a player lands nearby and grabs a weapon first, they'll have a huge advantage, unless you take cover and can stay hidden from them until you're also armed.

You can always drop less-powerful weapons later from the Inventory screen. At the start of a match, it's essential to arm yourself with whichever weapon(s) you can grab the quickest. Possessing a weak gun is far better than having no gun when you're being shot at and need to fight back.

Very early in a match, don't worry too much about grabbing items aside from weapons and ammo. If enemies collect other items that are nearby but they are not well armed, they'll be easy to kill, and you'll be able to take the items you want from their corpses after you've killed them.

#2—TAKE ADVANTAGE OF THE ALT LOOK FEATURE

When playing the PC version of *PUBG*, press and hold down the ALT key when you need to look around. This will allow you to look around your area in a way that's independent of the direction your soldier is facing. You can easily look all around you (360-degrees) without physically moving your soldier.

Use the ALT Look feature while freefalling to quickly determine whether or not enemy soldiers are close by and will be landing near you. You can also see where other soldiers land and then choose your exact landing spot accordingly.

Once your soldier lands, using ALT Look will allow you to spot enemies in all directions more easily, especially if you're out in the open and trying to avoid surprise attacks or ambushes. By determining where your enemies are, you can then select the most efficient way to attack and kill them quickly, or if you're not well armed, devise a strategy to avoid getting detected. A similar feature is offered within the other versions of *PUBG*, but it's controlled using the gaming system's controller.

#3—USE POWERFUL SCOPES AS BINOCULARS

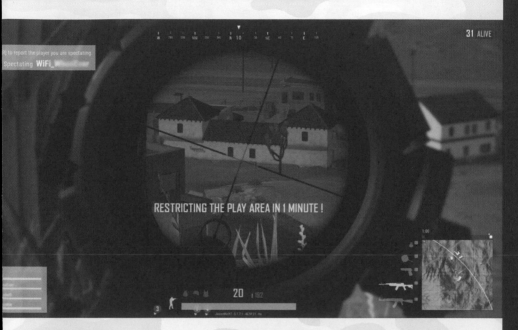

Knowing where your enemies are is essential. If you have a gun with a powerful Scope attached, use that Scope as binoculars to spot enemies at a great distance. Even if you're limited on ammo for that gun, simply knowing where your enemies are hiding while they're far away gives you the opportunity to plan an attack based on the weapons and ammo you have available. You can always move in closer, toss an explosive weapon to lure an enemy out into the open, or reposition yourself to a location that's better suited for sniping.

#4—A HEIGHT ADVANTAGE IS TYPICALLY BENEFICIAL

Regardless of where you are on the island, or how far into a match you are, when it comes to engaging in combat, having a height advantage over your opponent is almost always beneficial.

When applicable, climb or drive a vehicle to the top of a hill or mountain to get up higher than your enemies, so you can shoot down at them.

If you can get to the roof of a tall building or structure so you can shoot at enemies below, this too can work to your advantage, especially if you have access to a Sniper Rifle or a weapon with a powerful Scope that allows you to shoot with extreme accuracy from a distance.

In many areas, when buildings are close together, your soldier can leap from one roof to another in order to maintain a height advantage yet still move between buildings or structures.

#5—TAKE ADVANTAGE OF "CROUCH JUMPING" TO REACH CERTAIN AREAS

Simply by crouching down and jumping simultaneously, you're often able to reach areas that would otherwise be inaccessible if your soldier were standing up and jumping. For example, use a Crouch Jump to leap over short walls or to jump through an open window. Press the Jump button and Crouch button at the same time to achieve a Crouch Jump.

Use a Crouch Jump to quickly escape a building through a window when a heavily armed enemy is standing between you and the door, or an enemy is waiting outside a door to launch an attack. If you try to use a normal jump, your soldier will not fit through most windows.

#6—LOOK AND LISTEN BEFORE YOU ENTER

Before entering into any structure, especially if you notice the door is already open, as quietly as possible, sneak up to a window and peek through. If you spot any enemies, you can shoot at them through a window, or toss in an explosive weapon to clear the area before entering.

Just by standing outside of a building for a few seconds before entering, you'll often hear footsteps or other noises being generated if there are enemies lurking inside. Even if a door is closed, before entering, listen carefully for a few seconds to help determine if anyone is already inside.

#7—BEWARE OF OPEN DOORS

By default, all doors to structures and buildings are closed at the start of a match. If you notice an open door, this means that an enemy has already entered into that structure and may still be inside.

Listen closely for sounds from the enemy soldier and proceed inside with extreme caution. It's a common strategy for soldiers to crouch down behind an object within a structure and wait to ambush enemies that enter after them.

If you want to confuse your enemies and launch your own surprise ambushes, be sure to close all doors behind you after passing through them.

#8—MAKE YOUR SOLDIER HOLD THEIR BREATH WHILE SHOOTING

Having your soldier hold their breath when shooting increases their aiming accuracy. On most gaming systems, an animated lungs icon will be displayed to the right of your soldier's Health meter when they're holding their breath. If they hold their breath for too long, it'll take them a few seconds to recover, which temporarily slows them down when it comes to aiming, shooting, and reloading their weapon.

Once your soldier holds their breath for too long, they won't be able to run at all until they've had time to breath air back into their lungs, so plan accordingly. Until your lungs are fully replenished with air, the amount of time you can hold your breath again will be diminished.

#9—LEARN HOW TO SWITCH SEATS IN A VEHICLE

Most types of vehicles available in *PUBG* have several different seats for passengers. If you're riding in a vehicle when a partner or squad mate is driving, switching seats can often give you a better angle or perspective when shooting at enemies. If you're the sole driver of a vehicle that's being attacked, if you jump out of the driver's seat and exit the vehicle, an enemy will be able to anticipate this move and kill you more easily. However, if you leap to another seat on the opposite side from where the vehicle is being attacked, you can exit the vehicle in another direction, which gives you time to shoot back or escape on foot. The vehicle will also provide extra cover.

#10—TAKE ADVANTAGE OF A VEHICLE'S SPEED BOOST CAPABILITY

By filling up your soldier's Boost meter, while driving in many types of vehicles, if you hold down the Shift key (PC version), while also pressing on the gas pedal button or key, this will give the vehicle a temporary speed boost, which is useful if you need to escape an area quickly or avoid an incoming attack. Keep in mind, however, that using the boost feature causes fuel to get used up much faster.

#11—PUT AWAY YOUR WEAPON WHEN RUNNING

If you need to cover a lot of territory quickly while traveling on foot, your soldier will be able to run faster if they holster their weapon, as opposed to carrying it. The drawback to this strategy is that it takes longer to draw, aim, load, and shoot a gun if you suddenly find yourself under attack and need to shoot back. Drinking an Energy Drink is another way to temporarily boost your soldier's running speed. (On a PC, press the X button to put your weapon away while running.)

Your soldier will be able to draw their Pistol faster than other types of weapons that have been stored while they're running. If you anticipate needing to run great distances, and achieving top speed is essential, consider carrying a Pistol so you can access it quickly if needed.

During the late stages of a match, you're better off keeping an Assault Rifle (set to Auto Fire) in hand when running around, since you're very likely to encounter well-armed enemies and will need to attack quickly.

#12—MANAGE YOUR INVENTORY, DON'T JUST COLLECT IT

Finding and collecting weapons, ammo, armor, weapon enhancements, and other items is an important element of *PUBG*. However, it's important to properly manage your inventory, as opposed to simply grabbing and collecting everything you encounter.

Manage your soldier's inventory from the Inventory screen, but make sure your soldier is in a secure location before you switch to this screen and take your attention away from what's happening around you during a match.

To free up as much inventory space a possible, attach weapon enhancements to compatible weapons you're carrying, and only carry around items you believe you'll need as you go further in the match. Drop items you no longer need.

Knowing that the longer you survive during a match, the greater your chances are of encountering enemies that you'll need to fight, always keep an ample supply of Health replenishment items (Bandages, First Aid Kits, and Med Kits) with you.

Painkillers and Energy Drinks are also important items to have during the later stages of a match to help you move faster and stay alive longer, so be sure you have room for them in your inventory.

Be sure you collect and carry an ample supply of ammunition for your most powerful weapons and the weapons that you're most proficient at using. Carrying too much ammo for less powerful weapons, for example, takes away from the inventory space you'll need for medical supplies and health items.

Grabbing and wearing a level 3 Backpack increases the amount of inventory you can carry, so it's always beneficial to grab and upgrade to a level 3 Backpack as soon as you encounter one.

Once you drop and dispose of any weaker weapons you no longer want or need, drop the ammo you have for that weapon as well. Doing this will free up more inventory space so your soldier can carry more ammo for the weapons you deem the most useful or most powerful.

#13—CHOOSE A REMOTE AREA TO LAND

If you want to stay alive longer and run into far fewer enemies during the early stages of a match, choose to land in a remote area. The drawback is that these remote areas often have a worse selection of weapons, ammo, armor, weapon enhancements, and items to collect. The benefit is that you have more time to build up your arsenal before being forced into combat.

Many gamers typically opt to have their soldiers leap from the aircraft early on its path across the island. Simply by waiting until the plane has almost reached the end of its flight path, you're virtually guaranteed to encounter fewer enemies at the start of a match. The problem is, to stay within the safe area of the island once the blue wall starts to expand, you may wind up having to travel much greater distances.

As the airplane is flying over the island, following the route that's depicted on the map with a line, pay attention to the airplane's seating chart (which in the PC version is displayed on the left side of the map screen). Each dot represents one occupied aircraft seat. When a dot turns black, this means a soldier has jumped from the plane. Keeping an eye on the seating chart is one way to determine when and where large numbers of enemy soldiers are exiting the aircraft.

If you exit the plane directly over your desired landing spot, use the directional arrows to point your soldier straight down, so they fall faster and in a straight line downward. However, if you want to glide a bit in midair, keep your soldier's body parallel to the land, or manually activate their parachute early, so you have more precise navigational control during the fall. Keep your falling speed under 130kph to maximize the distance you can travel.

#14—ASSAULT RIFLES ARE EXCELLENT GENERAL-PURPOSE WEAPONS

There are many different types of guns available in *PUBG* and new weapons are continuously being added to the game. If you're an average-skilled player, one of the most versatile types of guns you always want at your disposal is an Assault Rifle. These are useful at any range. With weapon upgrades, you can improve the aim accuracy and ammo capacity of these weapons.

#15—PAY ATTENTION TO YOUR SOLDIER'S BOOST BAR

Located directly above your soldier's Health bar, when applicable, is their Boost bar. This yellow bar has four sections. Using Pain Killers and Energy Drinks, for example, will fill your soldier's Boost bar. Adding to your soldier's Boost bar allows them run and heal faster.

The first two lines of the Boost bar allow your soldier to heal faster, while the third line temporarily increases your soldier's running speed.

#16—DON'T TAKE UNNECESSARY RISKS

There will be many opportunities during a match where you can take a risk in order to achieve extra kills or acquire additional and useful weapons or items. Since your primary goal is to survive until the very end of the match so you become the last soldier alive, taking unnecessary risks can be detrimental to your health. If you take a risk and fail, more often than not, you'll wind up dead. Only take risks when it's absolutely necessary and the payoff outweighs the chance that your soldier will get injured or be killed.

#17—LET YOUR ENEMIES KILL EACH OTHER

Anytime you notice two enemy soldiers fighting each other, hide and watch the battle ensue. Wait for one soldier to kill the other and then approach the corpse of the loser to collect their bounty. While the victorious soldier is focused on grabbing what was left behind by their victim, launch a surprise attack, kill the surviving soldier, and then collect everything that both soldiers were carrying.

#18—SNIPE AT ENEMIES THAT APPROACH A CRATE DROP

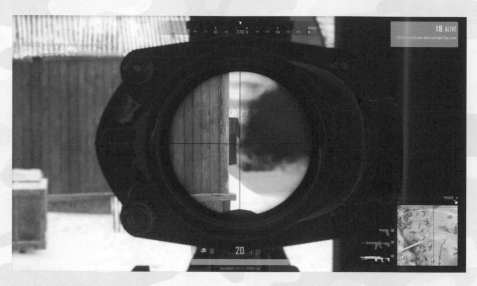

Anytime you see a Crate Drop you should get close to its anticipated landing spot and hide—preferably at a location that's higher up than where the crate lands. Use a Sniper Rifle or weapon with a Scope to pick off any enemy soldiers that approach the crate once it lands. Then once the area is clear, collect what you can from the fallen soldier(s) as well as from the crate itself.

Crate Drops are dropped randomly and always contain the best and most powerful guns, armor, and weapon enhancements within them. The problem is that Crate Drops attract a lot of attention, because all surviving soldiers typically want what's in them. If you're a newb, you're better off leaving Crate Drops alone, because you'll typically need to fight at least one enemy (sometimes several) in order to get away alive with the items the Crate Drop contains.

The best Sniper Rifle in the game (the AWM), along with the M249 (a light machine gun), and Tommy Gun (an SMG), are among the guns that can only be found within crates. You'll also discover level 3 armor within Crate Drops, as well as Adrenaline Syringes (which are another Crate Drop exclusive). These take 10 seconds to work but increase your soldier's Boost meter to 100 percent.

#19—PAY ATTENTION TO THE MAP

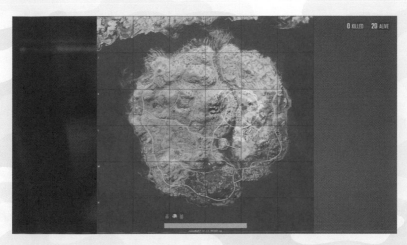

Enemy soldiers are one of the biggest threats on the island, but don't discount the danger imposed by the blue wall. When viewing the map screen, inside the circle is the current safe area on the island. The white circle shows how much the blue wall will be shrinking next and where the safe area will be once the blue wall moves and shrinks again. This is vital information, because if you get caught in the unsafe area of the island (outside of the blue wall) for too long, you'll wind up dead.

Anytime you're on the wrong side of the blue wall, you'll see blood splats on the screen. However, if you're on the inside of the blue wall and keep your back close to it, you can put a lot more focus on what's happening in front and to the sides of your soldier, as opposed to what's happening behind them.

It's rare for an enemy to venture into the unsafe side of the circle in order to launch a surprise attack, but it could happen. If your Health meter is full, you could sneak behind the blue wall and then remerge into the safe area of the island directly behind an enemy to launch a surprise attack. Should you choose to do this, make sure you pay attention to your Health meter and how long you have before the blue wall moves again.

Anytime you're out in the open and you hear an enemy approaching that you want to avoid, try hiding your entire body within a nearby bush (as opposed to behind a bush). During the final stages of a match, if you can't find where your enemy is hiding, shoot into bushes or throw projectile explosives at the nearby bushes to lure them out, since this is a commonly used hiding spot. Here the soldier is lying within a bush, but his legs and feet are exposed. A better option would be to crouch down in the bush, so the soldier's entire body is engulfed by the leaves and branches.

As you're hiding within a bush, press the ALT key (on the keyboard) to look around while preventing your soldier from physically moving. This will prevent the bush from shaking as a result of your movement, so you won't accidently give away your hiding place.

Lying flat on the grass is also a way to keep from being seen, plus make your soldier a harder target to hit, especially from a distance. If you lie down, tall grass offers a decent hiding space, but this can be risky. If you have your game's display resolution set higher than your opponent's, the density of the tall grass will appear to you more robust than it actually is. In other words, your opponent might not see the lushness of the grass and easily be able to spot you trying to hide. Tall grass also offers absolutely no shielding from bullets or explosions. For shielding, hide behind a tree, rock, wall, vehicle, or other solid object.

#20—SPRINT, DON'T WALK!

More often than not, when you're moving around on foot throughout the island, you'll want to sprint (run) as opposed to walk. Sprinting makes a little more noise than walking, but it allows you to reach your destination quickly, and helps to ensure you're a fast-moving target that's difficult for enemies to shoot at.

#21—WHEN PLAYING DUO OR SQUAD MATCHES, YOU NEED TO COMMUNICATE

Anytime you're experiencing a match with a partner or squad mates, clear communication is essential if you want to pull off well-coordinated attacks. Keep your communication brief, however. Focus on sharing only the information that's immediately necessary. This often includes details about nearby enemies. Be sure to share the enemy's **distance**, **direction**, and **description** as quickly as possible.

When sharing direction, don't use phrases like "ahead of," "in front of," "behind," "to the left," or "to the right." Unless you know your partner or squad mates are facing the same direction as you, these directional phrases are worthless. Instead, share directional information using the compass that's displayed near the top center of the screen. For example, say "Enemy is North, 50 meters ahead, within the house's second floor." This provides the core information needed about an enemy and their position.

Also, if you're planning on taking a specific action against an enemy, in addition to sharing the enemy's distance, direction, and description, quickly summarize and share with your partner or squad mates what you're about to do and how you're going to do it.

If you're going to push an enemy, for example, either ask your partner or squad mates to accompany you, flank the enemy from different directions, or stay back and provide cover fire, for example. Make sure everyone knows and agrees upon what they should do to successfully execute a well-coordinated and perfectly timed attack.

When playing a Duo or Squad game with strangers who you've been matched up with, instead of referring to each other by name during a match, save time by referring to each other by the color used to depict them on the mini-map and map screen. This saves time and confusion, especially if you have trouble remembering or pronouncing peoples' names.

#22—DON'T FORGET YOU HAVE MANY RESPONSIBILITIES DURING EACH MATCH

Even if your goal is to achieve as many kills as possible during each match, a lot of your time will still be spent traveling in between locations to avoid the blue wall, as well as finding and collecting weapons, ammo, armor, and loot items. Don't ignore these other important elements of the game. Focus on all of your soldier's responsibilities during each match, not just the tasks you enjoy or are the best at.

#23—IF YOU'RE PLAYING A DUO OR SQUAD MATCH, STICK TOGETHER

Anytime you're playing a Duo or Squad match and your partner or squad mates are still alive, stick together. This allows you to watch each other's back, work together on offensive strategies, and heal each other if someone gets injured.

Sharing weapons, ammo, armor, and loot items is also beneficial. Assign one player to collect items while the other(s) stand guard, for example. It's much easier to survive as a team or squad if everyone remains well armed during a match.

When sharing items or ammo, you're able to share a portion of what you're holding, as opposed to your entire stash of that item.

In addition, while driving in a vehicle, the driver is unable to drive and fire a weapon at the same time. However, a passenger of the vehicle can ride and shoot simultaneously.

Meanwhile, if one player needs to heal their soldier, using a Med Kit or First Aid Kit, for example (which takes several seconds), a team member or squad mate can stand guard and offer protection.

When traveling on foot with one or more soldiers, don't stay too close together. Groups of two, three, or four soldiers standing or traveling in close proximity are much easier targets to hit, especially with an explosive weapon.

#24—NEVER STAND STILL WHILE LOOTING

Whether you're having your soldier collect items from a corpse, opening a Crate Drop, or picking up loot within a building or structure, keep moving as much as possible. As soon as you stand still for more than a second or two, you make yourself an easy target for enemies. A moving target is always a harder target to kill than a soldier who is standing still.

Looting a dead soldier, especially during the final stages of a match, takes time and often puts you out in the open and makes you an easier target. Unless you absolutely need to replenish your arsenal or require loot items to ensure your survival, sometimes it's best to leave the dead soldiers alone and forego looking for their corpses.

#25—TAKE ADVANTAGE OF THE AUTO-RUN FEATURE

Anytime you need to travel a long distance on foot take advantage of the Auto-Run feature so your soldier will keep running in the direction you select without you having to hold down the Run/Sprint button. While using Auto-Run, you can still look around and watch out for enemies.

The Auto-Run feature also works nicely while swimming.

#26—CHOOSE YOUR FIGHTS CAREFULLY

Even if you spot an enemy that could be an easy kill, if you know there are a lot of enemies in the area (especially during the later stages of a match), by firing your weapon, you'll be alerting all of the nearby enemies to your position. Make sure executing that extra kill is worth the risk. Letting your enemies kill each other allows you to stay in the match longer.

#27—ROCKS, TREES, AND BUSHES ARE GREAT TO HIDE BEHIND

While you're hiding safely in a bush (or another hiding spot) and can't be seen by nearby enemies, don't reveal your position by firing your weapon in order to achieve a kill, unless you need to protect yourself. Determine what your priorities are during each stage of a match, and then act accordingly without allowing your emotions or greed to interfere with your safety.

Trees and rocks offer great cover if you have your soldier hide behind them.

#28—USE EXPLOSIVE GRENADES DURING THE LATE STAGES OF A MATCH

If you manage to be one of the final few soldiers alive during the end game portion of a match, where all of the surviving soldiers are in very close proximity, tossing Grenades not only will help you lure enemies out of hiding, but the explosions could allow you to injure or kill multiple enemies at once who are very close together.

#29—IF YOU GET INJURED WHILE IN WATER, TRY TO REACH LAND QUICKLY

A healthy soldier can easily swim in water. You'll find your soldier can swim faster while totally submerged underwater, as opposed to at the water's surface.

However, an injured soldier will quickly drown. Don't waste the time trying to heal your soldier if they are submerged. You're better off trying to reach land first before using any healing items. If you're playing a Duo or Squad match, it's always a better idea to revive a team mate or squad mate on land, as opposed to within water.

When you need to run through water, try crouching as opposed to standing upright while running. This often increases your travel speed.

#30—CONSIDER DROPPING YOUR SOLDIER'S BACKPACK DURING THE END GAME

During the final stages of a match, if you no longer need the items stored within your soldier's Backpack, drop the Backpack. This makes your soldier's profile a bit slimmer, which means that when they're lying on the ground or hiding behind a narrow object (like a tree), they'll be more difficult to spot.

PUBG ONLINE RESOURCES

O N YOUTUBE (WWW.YOUTUBE.COM) OR TWITCH.TV (WWW.TWITCH.TV), IN THE Search field, enter the search phrase *"PUBG"* or *"PlayerUnknown Battlefields"* to discover many game-related channels, live streams, and prerecorded videos that'll help you become a better player.

USEFUL PUBG RESOURCES

To keep up-to-date on all of the latest *PUBG* news and updates, plus discover even more strategies, be sure to check out these online resources:

WEBSITE OR YOUTUBE CHANNEL NAME	DESCRIPTION	URL
Corsair	One of several manufacturers of top-quality keyboards, headsets, and mice used by skilled PUBG gamers.	http://corsair.com/us/en
Game Informer Magazine's *PUBG* Coverage	Discover articles, reviews, and news about *PUBG* published by *Game Informer* magazine.	www.gameinformer. com (Within the Search field for this website, enter PUBG.)
Game Skinny Online Guides	A collection of topic-specific strategy guides related to *PUBG*.	www.gameskinny.com (Within the Search field for this website, enter PUBG.)
GameSpot's *PUBG* Coverage	Check out the news, reviews, and game coverage related to *PUBG* that's been published by GameSpot.	www.gamespot.com (Within the Search field for this website, enter PUBG.)
IGN Entertainment's *PUBG* Coverage	Check out all IGN's past and current coverage of *PUBG*.	www.ign.com (Within the Search field for this website, enter PUBG.)
Jason R. Rich's Website and Social Media Feeds	Share your *PUBG* game play strategies with this book's author and learn about his other books.	www.JasonRich.com www.GameTipBooks .com Twitter: @JasonRich7 Instagram: @JasonRich7

Microsoft's PUBG Webpage for Xbox One Version	The official webpage from Microsoft covering *PUBG* for the Xbox One game console	www.xbox.com/ en-US/games/ playerunknowns-battlegrounds
Official *PUBG* Online Support	Get questions to commonly asked questions answered and seek out *PUBG*-related support online.	www.pubg.com/support
Official *PUBG* Website	PlayerUnknown's Official *PUBG* website.	www.pubg.com
PlayerUnknown Battlegrounds Wiki	An unofficial resource related to all things *PUBG*	http://pubg.gamepedia. com
PUBG Strategies	An unofficial website containing useful *PUBG* news and tips.	www.pubgstrategies. com
PUBG Tips	An unofficial webpage containing useful *PUBG* news and tips.	http:// pubattlegroundstips. com
PUBGMap.io	An unofficial and independent *PUBG* website that offers detailed island maps, along with information about the game's current weapons, armor, ammo, and loot items.	http://pubgmap.io
Razer	One of several manufacturers of top-quality keyboards, headsets, and mice used by top PUBG gamers.	www.razer.com
Sony PlayStation's *PUBG* Webpage for the PS4	The official webpage from Sony covering *PUBG* for the PS4 game console.	www.playstation. com/en-us/games/ playerunknowns-battlegrounds-ps4
The Official PlayerUnknown's YouTube Channel for *PUBG*	The official *PUBG* YouTube channel.	www.youtube.com/ pubg

(Continued on next page)

The official *PUBG* Social Media Accounts	These are the social media accounts for PlayerUnknown that relate to *PUBG*.	Facebook: www.facebook.com/PUBG Twitter: www.twitter.com/PUBG Instagram: www.instagram.com/pubg
Turtle Beach Corp.	This is one of many companies that make great quality, wired or wireless (Bluetooth) gaming headsets that work with all gaming platforms.	www.turtlebeach.com

YOUR *PUBG* ADVENTURE CONTINUES . . .

There are many compelling reasons why *PUBG* has become a worldwide phenomenon, as opposed to just another popular game. Thanks to new map locations, new weapons, new loot items, and other interesting gaming features regularly being added, there are always new places to visit and new things to try.

More importantly, because you're always competing against up to 99 other human gamers, even the most experienced and highly skilled *PUBG* players never know for sure what to expect. As a result, every match you experience will be unique, and you'll often face a different assortment of challenges and obstacles.

Even if you've been playing for a while yet haven't been able to win a match and earn a much-coveted chicken dinner, this does not necessarily mean you're a bad player. It simply means you need additional practice. Try to determine where your weaknesses lie, and then learn to compensate for them by spending more time using Training Mode.

Another really useful way to learn from other skilled players is to participate in Squad matches and choose the auto-matching feature, so you're teamed up with strangers. You'll sometimes wind up playing with a highly skilled and experienced gamer from whom you can learn a lot. Also, after losing a match, take advantage of the Spectator mode, so you can study how the players who were previously your adversaries manage to survive the match.

Try to avoid getting frustrated each time you get killed. Learn from your mistakes and keep entering into new matches. The more time you spend on the island, the more comfortable you'll become navigating around what will soon become familiar terrain. Developing a strong knowledge of the terrain will help you find valuable weapons, ammo, armor, and loot items faster, quickly choose the best places to launch attacks from, and easily locate the best places to hide or take cover when you're being shot at.

Finally, if you're having trouble achieving the results you desire, even after developing a strong understanding of the game, take the time to make small changes to the game controls, and consider upgrading your controller, keyboard, and/or mouse to one that offers greater precision.

Also, see what you can do about improving your Internet speed. If you're using a PC or console-based system, establishing a wired connection to your modem, as opposed to relying on a wireless Wi-Fi connection, could give you a subtle speed boost that's enough to positively impact your gaming performance.

Most importantly, anytime you're playing *PUBG*, focus on having fun!